HOT DOG DIARY

HOT DOG DIARY

NATHAN TOLZMANN

BOATWHISTLE BOOKS

FIRST PUBLISHED IN 2022
BY BOATWHISTLE BOOKS
22 GLOUCESTER ROAD
TWICKENHAM
LONDON TW2 6NE
UNITED KINGDOM

WWW.BOATWHISTLE.COM

© NATHAN TOLZMANN 2022

A CATALOGUE RECORD FOR THIS BOOK
IS AVAILABLE FROM THE BRITISH LIBRARY

ISBN 978-1-911052-08-1

PRINTED IN THE UNITED KINGDOM BY TJ BOOKS OF PADSTOW,
ON 80 GSM FSC-CERTIFIED MUNKEN PREMIUM PAPER

This is what I thought: for the most banal event to become an adventure, you must (and this is enough) begin to recount it. This is what fools people: a man is always a teller of tales, he lives surrounded by his stories and the stories of others, he sees everything that happens to him through them; and he tries to live his own life as if he were telling a story.

But you have to choose: live or tell.

JEAN-PAUL SARTRE

Introduction

Prologue

Hot Dog Diary

DENVER TO SAN FRANCISCO **July 17**

SAN FRANCISCO **July 18**

SAN FRANCISCO **July 19**

Dan was a high school classmate of Matt's. I'd met him a couple of times. I'd never met his wife, Monya, before.

They let us sleep on their floor while we prepared ourselves for the trip.

Their neighborhood, Outer Sunset, isn't exactly in the heart of San Francisco, but it is right by Golden Gate Park. It was a beautiful Sunday so Dan, Matt and I walked through the park and then on to the Musée Mécanique located in the Cliff House.

"Wasn't Pat supposed to go on the bike trip too?"

The Musée Mécanique is a penny arcade. You can see miniature dolls re-enact a French execution and an English execution. You can see "Laughing Sal" bust a gut. She laughs and laughs. The laughter is contagious until she makes a spectacle of herself.

"He decided not to come."

"When is she going to stop?"

WHEN WE'D HAD OUR FILL OF PUTTING COINS IN SLOTS WE LEFT AND CHECKED OUT THE CAMERA OBSCURA LOCATED NEARBY.

ONE DOLLAR BOUGHT ENTRY INTO A ROOM-SIZED CAMERA. A PINHOLE AND MIRROR ON TOP OF THE BUILDING CONTINUOUSLY, SLOWLY TURNING PROJECTING THE IMAGE ONTO A CIRCULAR SCREEN IN THE MIDDLE OF THE ROOM.

THE IMAGE WAS SO CLEAR, YET SOFT. THE GLARE FROM THE WATER WAS TRANSFORMED INTO A TWINKLING SPARKLE.

PEOPLE IN DAVINCI'S DAY WERE CAPTIVATED BY THE EFFECT. TO MODERN EYES IT'S LIKE SOME SORT OF MOVIE OR LIVE-STREAMED VIDEO. WHAT COULD THEY COMPARE IT TO? I'VE SEEN TV AND MOVIES MY WHOLE LIFE BUT I WAS CAPTIVATED STILL.

SAN FRANCISCO **July 20**

We figured we'd have lots of time for reading once we started biking so we headed downtown to find a bookstore.

Why hadn't we already chosen books for the trip? I guess with all the other preparations it hadn't seemed a priority.

"We should each pick one book"

"And then when we finish them we can trade"

Now there was a lot of pressure to choose correctly. Anything extra in stowage had to be justified. The books we picked were going to have to carry their weight.

"Blue Highways this would be great to read on a trip"

"Walk Across America would be a good one too"

"But we've already read both of those"

SAN FRANCISCO **July 22**

BERKELEY **July 23**

WE TOOK BAY AREA RAPID TRANSIT TO BERKELEY TO VISIT MATT'S AUNT

ARLENE PICKED US UP AT THE STATION. MATT'S ACHINESS HADN'T GONE AWAY AND NOW HIS THROAT HAD STARTED TO HURT. HOPEFULLY SLEEPING IN A BED AND HAVING A RELATIVE TO LOOK AFTER HIM WOULD BE GOOD MEDICINE.

I WANT TO SHOW YOU THE TOY STORE

ARLENE WAS A RETIRED SCHOOL TEACHER. NOW SHE WORKED PART TIME AT A USED TOY STORE CALLED TOY GO ROUND THAT SHE WAS VERY EXCITED ABOUT

THERE'S A MUSEUM I WANT TO TAKE YOU TO

THE JUDAH L. MAGNES MUSEUM HAD AN EXHIBIT CALLED "SOUVENIRS FROM ISRAEL 1948-1998". TO COMMEMORATE ISRAEL'S 50TH ANNIVERSARY THE MUSEUM HAD COLLECTED THINGS THAT PEOPLE IN THE BAY AREA JEWISH COMMUNITY HAD BROUGHT BACK FROM THE HOLY LAND. MEMENTOS AT THE CONFLUENCE OF TOURISM AND PILGRIMAGE.

WE MET MATT'S COUSIN AT THE BOOKSTORE. LEANN WAS FROM MISSOULA BUT WAS LIVING IN CALIFORNIA AT THE TIME. CODY'S BOOKS HAD A LONG-RUNNING AUTHOR-READING SERIES AND WAS ALSO NOTABLE FOR HAVING BEEN FIREBOMBED IN 1989, PRESUMABLY FOR SELLING SALMAN RUSHDIE'S SATANIC VERSES

OAKLAND **July 25**

WITH PENICILLIN IN HIS SYSTEM MATT WAS NOW ON THE MEND. THE TRIP WAS GOING TO BE DIFFICULT IN GOOD HEALTH LET ALONE SICKNESS SO WE CONTINUED TO DELAY OUR DEPARTURE UNTIL HE WAS FULLY ABLE. A VISIT TO THE OAKLAND MUSEUM OF CALIFORNIA WAS A GOOD WAY TO SPEND SOME RECUPERATIVE TIME. ON EXHIBIT WAS A SHOW COMMEMORATING THE SESQUICENTENNIAL OF THE START OF THE CALIFORNIA GOLD RUSH IN 1848

"HEY, LOOK AT THIS ONE"

I have seen the elephant

THE MOST USEFUL THING WE LEARNED AT THE EXHIBIT WAS THE PHRASE "I HAVE SEEN THE ELEPHANT"

APPARENTLY IT WAS A PRETTY COMMON IDIOM IN THE 19TH CENTURY. SOLDIERS WRITING HOME FROM THE CIVIL WAR USED IT TO SIGNIFY THAT THEY HAD SEEN COMBAT. PIONEERS AND FORTUNE-SEEKERS HEADING WEST WROTE EXPECTANTLY ABOUT THE MOMENT WHEN THEY WOULD FINALLY SEE THE ELEPHANT. AT THE SAME TIME THEY DESCRIBED HARDSHIPS ENDURED ALONG THE WAY AS MOMENTS WHEN THEY HAD SEEN THE ELEPHANT.

A fable from the time told of a farmer who found that a traveling circus was to be bringing an elephant to his town. Never having seen an elephant, and having a great desire to see one, he hitched horse to wagon, filled it with produce for the market, and headed to town.

On the way he and his horse happened to cross paths with the circus wagons. He and his horse saw the elephant at the same time, but with wildly different reactions. He was amazed. His horse was spooked, turned over the wagon, dumped the farmer and the produce on the ground, and ran off.

BERKELEY **July 26**

MATT AND DAVID WERE BEST FRIENDS IN GRADE SCHOOL. DAVID MOVED AWAY IN 7TH GRADE AND MATT HADN'T SEEN HIM SINCE. A JOB AT THE STAR TRIBUNE A FEW YEARS BACK HAD ALLOWED MATT RARE ACCESS TO THE WORLD WIDE WEB. MATT DISCOVERED THAT THE NATION'S PHONE BOOKS COULD BE SEARCHED ONLINE SO HE STARTED TO LOOK FOR DAVID. HE FOUND HIM AND THEY STRUCK UP A CORRESPONDENCE

MATT REACHED OUT TO DAVID TO LET HIM KNOW THAT WE'D BE IN NORTHERN CALIFORNIA SO MAYBE THEY COULD PLAN A REUNION. DAVID MADE THE DRIVE DOWN FROM DAVIS AND WE MET UP WITH HIM AT A KITE FESTIVAL

MAYBE IT WAS ODD THAT I, A STRANGER TO DAVID, WAS THERE FOR THE REUNION, BUT WERE THEY MUCH MORE THAN STRANGERS AT THIS POINT THEMSELVES? SOMETIMES YOU CAN PICK RIGHT BACK UP WHERE YOU LEFT OFF, BUT THEY HAD LEFT OFF IN SEVENTH GRADE. THAT'S A TOUGH TIME TO PICK BACK UP FROM.

WE MADE SMALL TALK AND MARVELLED AT THE AMAZING KITES. THEN WE NOTICED A MAN FLYING THREE DOUBLE-LINE KITES. HE HAD THEM PERFORMING ALL SORTS OF FANTASTIC STUNTS. TO MASTER THESE KITE-FLYING SKILLS THE GUY HAD OBVIOUSLY SPENT A LOT OF TIME OUTSIDE PRACTICING. A LOT OF TIME UNDER THE CALIFORNIA SUN. A LOT OF TIME WITH NO SHIRT ON. THE GUY WAS A MASTER, BUT WE FOUND OURSELVES FOCUSING ON HOW LEATHERY HE LOOKED INSTEAD OF HIS KITE SKILLS. MAYBE THEY HAD PICKED UP WHERE THEY LEFT OFF AFTER ALL

SAN FRANCISCO **July 28**

SAN FRANCISCO TO SAMUEL TAYLOR STATE PARK, PT. REYES **July 29**

WE PASSED THE BRIDGE THAT WE WOULD RIDE OVER THE GOLDEN GATE TAKING US NORTHWARD AND ON OUR WAY, BUT FIRST WE HAD TO RETRIEVE THE STAMP

FINALLY BACK ON OUR WAY OUT OF THE CITY, ALREADY A LOT OF HILLS UNDER OUR BELT AND NOW THE WIND IN OUR FACE

IT WAS ALREADY LUNCH TIME BY THE TIME WE GOT TO SAUSALITO SO WE TOOK A BREAK AND ATE. WE SAT IN THE SUN LOOKING ACROSS THE BAY AT THE CLOUDS HANGING OVER SAN FRANCISCO. WE'D FINALLY MADE IT OUT! WE MADE SKETCHES OF THE BEAUTIFUL SCENE AND THEN IT WAS TIME TO PUT SOME MORE DISTANCE BETWEEN US AND THE CITY THAT HAD HELD US CAPTIVE SO LONG

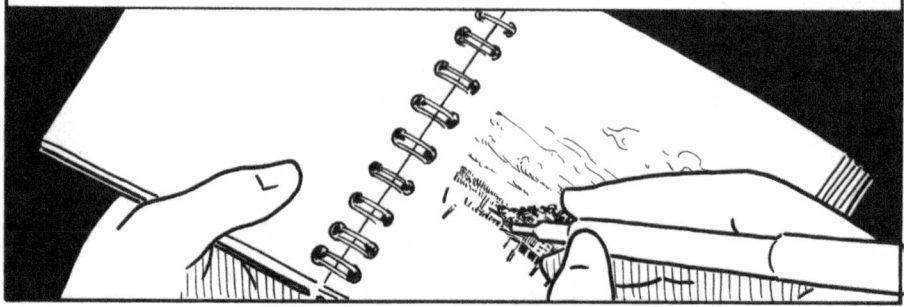

WE FOUND A BIKE TRAIL AND STARTED FOLLOWING IT

HI, DO YOU KNOW IF THIS WILL TAKE US TO HIGHWAY 1?

OH, YOU MISSED THE TURNOFF A WAYS BACK

WE'D HAD OUR FILL OF BACKTRACKING ALREADY SO WE JUST KEPT ON THE PATH UNTIL IT FIZZLED OUT IN A NEIGHBORHOOD. WE ASKED A JOGGER FOR DIRECTIONS AND SHE POINTED US IN THE RIGHT DIRECTION

AND THAT WILL TAKE YOU TO SIR FRANCIS DRAKE BOULEVARD

WE TOOK SIR FRANCIS DRAKE BOULEVARD THE REST OF THE DAY. AT TIMES THERE WAS A LOT OF TRAFFIC AND NO SHOULDER. SOMETIMES THE SHOULDER WAS WIDE AND SMOOTH AND THERE WAS NO TRAFFIC. THE ROAD WAS QUITE CONSISTENT IN ITS STEEPNESS AND CURVINESS THOUGH

IT WAS GETTING LATE. MATT WENT TO FIND CAMPING AND I RODE AHEAD INTO PT. REYES STATION TO PICK UP FOOD. I RODE BACK TO SAMUEL P. TAYLOR STATE PARK WITH THE GROCERIES, FOUND MATT, ATE, SHOWERED, AND FELL ASLEEP AS SOON AS I SLIPPED INTO MY SLEEPING BAG

PT REYES TO BODEGA DUNES CAMPGROUND, BODEGA BAY July 30

FOR SOME REASON WE HAD GOTTEN THE IDEA INTO OUR HEADS THAT THE SECOND DAY WOULD BE EASIER. IT WASN'T. IT WAS DRIZZLING IN THE MORNING. THE DRIZZLE LET UP, BUT THEN IT WAS GREY AND DAMP THE REST OF THE DAY. WE FOUGHT A HEAD WIND ON THE CURVING HILLS ALL DAY AND FINALLY MADE IT TO BODEGA BAY. THE FIRST CAMPSITE WE TRIED WAS FULL SO WE CONTINUED ON TO TRY OUT THE NEXT ONE UP THE ROAD. WHILE STOPPED AT A GROCERY STORE TO PICK UP PROVISIONS FOR OUR EVENING MEAL WE RAN INTO ANOTHER BIKER

"HAVE YOU COME ACROSS A RUNNER NAMED RYAN? HE'S RUNNING DOWN THE COAST. I'M SUPPOSED TO MEET HIM FOR BEERS AND SHARE A MOTEL ROOM WITH HIM TONIGHT"

"NO, WE HAVEN'T SEEN HIM"

"YOU GUYS CAN GO IN ON THE ROOM WITH US IF YOU WANT"

WE CONSIDERED HIS OFFER BUT STAYING IN A MOTEL ON ONLY OUR SECOND NIGHT ON THE ROAD SEEMED PREMATURE. IT PROBABLY WOULD'VE BEEN PRETTY CHEAP TO SPLIT THE ROOM WITH THEM, BUT WE WERE EVEN CHEAPER THAN THAT SO WE THANKED HIM FOR THE OFFER AND CONTINUED ON TO THE NEXT CAMPGROUND

BODEGA DUNE WAS FULL TOO, BUT THEY DID HAVE A HIKE/BIKE AREA SO WE WERE IN LUCK. BIKERS AND HIKERS DON'T NEED PARKING SPACES SO A LOT OF CAMPSITES HAVE AN AREA SET ASIDE WITH SOME TABLES AND FIRE PITS. THEN THEY FILL IT UP WITH HIKERS AND BIKERS AT FIVE BUCKS A HEAD. THERE WERE A LOT OF FELLOW TRAVELERS TO MEET

BODEGA BAY TO SALT POINT STATE PARK, OCEAN GROVE — July 31

WHEN WE LEFT CAMP THE ONLY ONES STILL THERE WERE RYAN AND THE TARP HERMIT. RYAN WAS GOING TO TAKE A DAY OFF ON ACCOUNT OF A PULLED HAMSTRING. IT WAS A BEAUTIFUL, SUNNY MORNING AND WE WERE REALLY ENJOYING THE BIKING. MAYBE THIS WILL BE THE EASY DAY WE HAD HOPED FOR

THE DETOUR TOOK US UP THE APTLY NAMED MEYERS GRADE ROAD

"THIS IS IMPOSSIBLE"

IN THE LOWEST GEAR AND STANDING ON THE PEDALS WE COULDN'T GET THE BIKES TO BUDGE. NOT WANTING TO HAVE TO PUSH OUR BIKES UP THE HILL AND NOT WANTING TO GET RUN OVER BY ALL OF THE GRAVEL TRUCKS TEARING UP AND DOWN THE ROAD, WE STOPPED TO THINK OVER OUR OPTIONS

"YOU SHOULD JUST TAKE HIGHWAY 1. IT'S CLOSED TO CARS, BUT I BET YOU COULD MAKE IT THROUGH ON BIKES"

"THANKS"

"IT'S WORTH A TRY"

There was an outbuilding with a tarp hanging over the front of it like a curtain. He pulled it aside and revealed his work. We chatted and he told us about his years working as a logger and a contracter and numerous other pursuits, and we talked about his art

We said goodbye and continued our climb. Reaching the top we were finally rewarded with a downhill. We flew down, tears streaming from our eyes. At the bottom we found a bar and grill to eat at and a place to camp

OCEAN GROVE TO MANCHESTER STATE PARK **August 1**

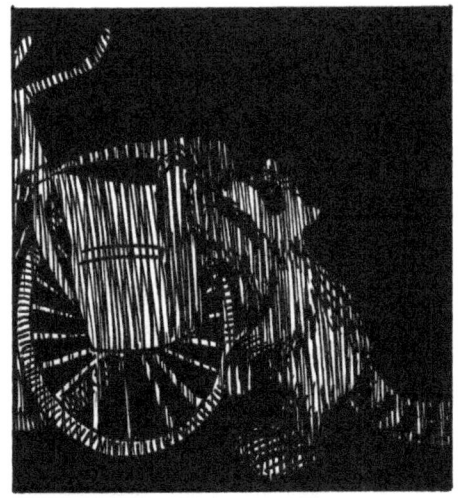

MANCHESTER TO WESTPORT-UNION LANDING STATE BEACH August 2

WE BID FAREWELL TO MARC AND KATY. WE WOULDN'T BE SEEING THEM AGAIN. WE HARDLY SAW ANY BIKERS TWICE. THIS WAS ONLY OUR FIFTH DAY ON THE BIKES, BUT IT HAD BECOME PRETTY CLEAR THAT ALMOST EVERYONE ELSE WAS TRAVELLING SOUTH. WE FOUGHT THE WINDS AND HILLS AGAIN UNTIL ELK WHEN WE SPOTTED A COOL SIGN

THESE DAYS OF BIKING AGAINST THE WIND ON HILLS WERE HARD ENOUGH WITHOUT BEING IN A BAD MOOD AND NOW I WAS IN A BAD MOOD. I RODE ALONG THINKING ABOUT WHAT I SHOULD'VE SAID TO HIM, BUT SNAPPY RETORTS AREN'T REALLY MY FORTÉ SO IT WAS POINTLESS TO KEEP DWELLING ON IT. AND YET I DID DWELL ON IT

I CONTINUED TO DWELL ON THIS LONELY OLD LONER WHO PROBABLY INTERACTED WITH OTHERS SO SELDOMLY THAT HE DIDN'T REMEMBER HOW TO BE DECENT. MAYBE HE NEVER KNEW. I WAS FRUSTRATED WITH MYSELF THAT I HADN'T SAID ANYTHING BACK TO HIM SO I TRIED TO CONVINCE MYSELF THAT IT HAD BEEN BEST TO JUST WALK AWAY.

THE THING IS THAT IT WOULDN'T HAVE BOTHERED ME SO MUCH IF I HAD HAD MORE CONFIDENCE IN WHAT I WAS DOING. HE WAS RIGHT. I HADN'T DONE MUCH BIKING, NOT LIKE THIS ANYWAY. WHEN OTHER BIKERS WOULD ASK US HOW FAR WE WERE GOING WE HAD TAKEN TO SAYING "PORTLAND." TO ADMIT OUR REAL GOAL WAS EMBARRASSING WHEN WE'D COVERED SO LITTLE DISTANCE SO FAR

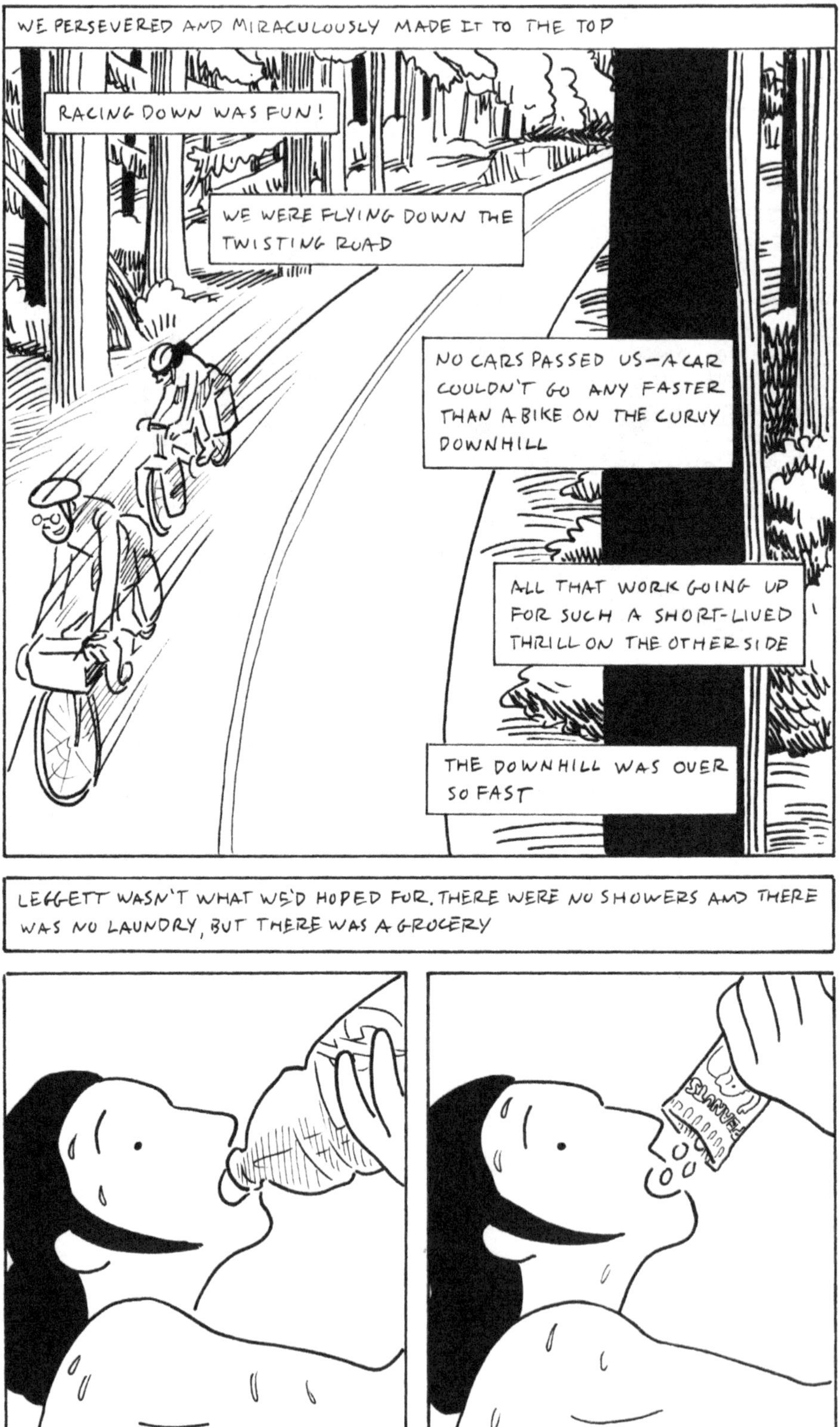

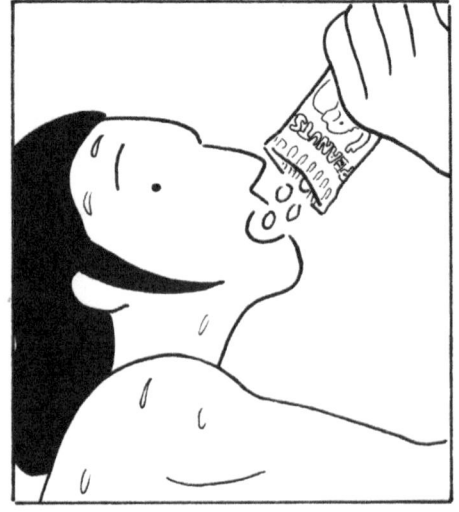

RICHARDSON GROVE S.P. TO HUMBOLDT REDWOODS S.P. **August 4**

AFTER THE GRUELING RIDE OF THE DAY BEFORE WE WERE NOT IN A HURRY TO GET BACK ON THE BIKES. WE STRUCK CAMP AND RODE INTO GARBERVILLE AND HAD A LEISURELY BREAKFAST AT THE EEL RIVER CAFE

AND THEN WE FOUND A LONG-HOPED-FOR LAUNDROMAT. WE EACH HAD 2 PAIRS OF BIKE SHORTS. AFTER A DAY OF BIKING WE'D WASH THE SHORTS IN A SINK...

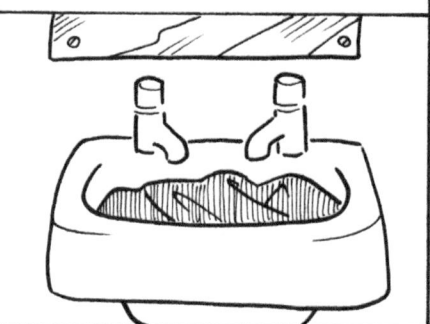

AND THEN THE NEXT DAY WE'D BUNGEE THEM ON THE BACK OF OUR BIKES FOR AN AIR DRY

ONE DAY ON ONE DAY OFF

THIS METHOD WORKED PRETTY WELL, BUT BY NOW THEY DESPERATELY NEEDED A SPIN CYCLE THAT WASN'T POSSIBLE WITH A SINK

HAVING A LAZY MORNING MEANT THAT BY THE TIME WE WERE READY TO GET BACK ON OUR WAY THE TEMPERATURE HAD CLIMBED UP PAST 100°. NOW THAT WE WERE ON THE REDWOOD HIGHWAY THERE WERE A LOT OF LOGGING TRUCKS BUT THERE WERE ALSO LOTS OF TOURIST ATTRACTIONS. WE STOPPED AT EVERY LOG HOUSE, CHIMNEY TREE, AND DRIVE-THROUGH TREE THAT WE SAW. THEY PROVIDED MUCH NEEDED BREAKS FROM THE HEAT AND FROM THE FEAR OF GETTING RUN OVER BY A LOGGING TRUCK

We left the Redwood Highway and started up the Avenue of the Giants. In Phillipsville we stopped at the famous "One-Log" House

I'm going to be retiring in 16 months. I'm hoping to sell, but if I can't find a buyer I'll just close it down. My kids grew up working in the gift shop, but they went off and got educated. None of them are interested in taking over

HUMBOLDT REDWOODS STATE PARK TO FORTUNA **August 5**

WE FOUND A SURPRISINGLY GOOD BREAKFAST AT THE IMMORTAL TREE HOUSE CAFE. THEN WE HEADED OUT, CONTINUING OUR PRACTICE FROM THE DAY BEFORE OF STOPPING AT EVERY GIFT SHOP ALONG THE WAY. IT WAS GOOD TO REMIND OURSELVES THAT WE WERE ON VACATION

WE PASSED THROUGH SCOTIA AND RIO DELL. SCOTIA IS A COMPANY TOWN OF THE PACIFIC LUMBER COMPANY (PALCO). IT WAS IMMACULATELY KEPT WITH NOTHING OUT OF PLACE. ITS SISTER CITY ACROSS THE RIVER WAS A DIFFERENT STORY

WE MADE IT TO FORTUNA AND COULD ONLY FIND CAMPING AT A KOA RIGHT BY THE FREEWAY, OUR TENT IN THE SHADOW OF A BEST WESTERN. NOT THE BEST CAMPSITE, BUT IT DID HAVE A HEATED POOL, HOT TUB, AND HOT SHOWERS WHICH WASN'T BAD

FORTUNA TO ARCATA **August 6**

MATT WAS PRETTY DISAPPOINTED THAT THERE WAS NO MAIL WAITING FOR HIM. WE WENT TO CARL'S FINE OMELETTES TO GET SOME BREAKFAST AND THEN MATT WENT BACK TO THE POST OFFICE TO CHECK AGAIN

WE WERE EXCITED TO GET TO ARCATA WHERE THERE WAS A HOSTEL. WE BLASTED THROUGH EUREKA AND GOT TO ARCATA HOURS BEFORE THE HOSTEL OPENED AT 5. IT FINALLY OPENED AND WE GOT A ROOM. THE MANAGER SHOWED US AROUND AND ASSIGNED US CHORES. I HAD TO VACUUM THE UPSTAIRS HALLWAY. IT TOOK ME ABOUT 2 MINUTES. MATT HAD TO SWEEP THE KITCHEN FLOOR. IT WAS PRETTY DIRTY.

ARCATA **August 7**

IT WAS NICE TO SLEEP IN A BED, BUT SLEEPING IN WASN'T REALLY AN OPTION BECAUSE WE HAD TO BE OUT OF THE HOSTEL FROM 9 TO 5. ONLY THE "PERMANENT RESIDENTS" WERE ALLOWED TO BE THERE DURING THAT TIME

WE'D BEEN BIKING FOR NINE DAYS AND WERE VERY READY FOR THIS PLANNED REST DAY. A BREAK FROM THE WIND AND THE HILLS AND THE TRAFFIC AND THE TRUCKS. WE DIDN'T HAVE TO TAKE DOWN THE TENT IN THE MORNING AND WE DIDN'T HAVE TO PUT IT BACK UP AGAIN AT NIGHT

MATT HADN'T BEEN ENJOYING THE TRIP VERY MUCH, BUT GETTING THE PACKAGE FROM HIS GIRLFRIEND SUE HAD IMPROVED HIS MOOD. INSTEAD OF THE CARE PACKAGE HE WAS EXPECTING SHE HAD SENT TOY WALKIE-TALKIES. USELESS, BUT FUNNY

WE THOUGHT WE'D HAVE TIME TO DO A LOT OF DRAWINGS ALONG THE WAY, BUT MOST OF OUR ENERGY WAS SPENT JUST GETTING FROM ONE POINT TO THE NEXT, SO WE TOOK THE OPPORTUNITY OF A FREE DAY TO SKETCH A LITTLE

MATT THOUGHT IT WOULDN'T BE THAT HARD TO FIND PUBLIC LIBRARIES WITH INTERNET ACCESS ALONG THE WAY SO HE COULD UPDATE HIS GEOCITIES WEBSITE ABOUT OUR TRIP. IT TURNED OUT TO BE HARD. IN ARCATA WE NEVER FOUND THE LIBRARY, BUT WE WANDERED AROUND THE SLEEPY UNIVERSITY CAMPUS, FOUND A COMPUTER, AND MATT WAS FINALLY ABLE TO POST AN UPDATE FROM THE ROAD

THERE WASN'T MUCH INTELLECTUAL STIMULATION WHILE BIKING. THE SAME THOUGHTS JUST TURNED OVER AND OVER IN OUR MINDS. PERHAPS A MOVIE WOULD INTRODUCE SOME NEW MATERIAL

"WELL, THAT'LL GIVE US SOMETHING TO THINK ABOUT FOR AWHILE"

WE DIDN'T GET TO HEAR MUCH MUSIC ASIDE FROM BACKGROUND MUSIC IN GIFT SHOPS AND RESTAURANTS SO IT WAS FUN TO SEE A LIVE BAND EVEN IF IT WAS SCARY HIPPIES PLAYING BLUEGRASS

THERE WERE A LOT OF HIPPIES IN TOWN, BUT THEY DIDN'T SEEM LIKE THE PEACE AND LOVE TYPE. THEY SEEMED TO BE MORE ON THE GUN-TOTING END OF THE HIPPIE SPECTRUM

BACK AT THE HOSTEL WE LEARNED ALL ABOUT THE SEASONAL POT FARMING WORK FROM A FELLOW GUEST

"YOU CAN MAKE ENOUGH MONEY IN 3 MONTHS TO LIVE OFF FOR THE REST OF THE YEAR"

"OH! THAT'S WHAT'S THE DEAL WITH THIS PLACE"

ARCATA TO PRAIRIE CREEK REDWOODS STATE PARK **August 8**

BREAK TIME OVER. IT WAS TIME TO START MOVING FORWARD AGAIN. WE PASSED THROUGH THE PICTURESQUE FISHING VILLAGE OF TRINIDAD

AND THEN SNAP! SOMETHING WAS WRONG WITH MY BIKE. THE PEDALS JUST SPUN

UH OH

BROKEN CHAIN!

HERE'S A LITTLE BON VOYAGE GIFT

IS A CHAIN BREAKER

I DOUBT YOU'D HAVE USE IT

BUT HERE'S A BIT OF CHAIN JUST IN CASE

FIXED IT!

PRAIRIE CREEK TO MILL CREEK CAMPGROUND **August 9**

WE ATE A LIGHT BREAKFAST IN CAMP FIGURING WE'D STOP FOR SOMETHING MORE SUBSTANTIAL SOON. THE ONLY RESTAURANT IN KLAMATH WAS A BAR SO WE WERE OUT OF LUCK. WE KEPT RIDING AND CAME ACROSS A GIFT SHOP THAT HAD A SMALL RESTAURANT ATTACHED

THEY HAD STOPPED SERVING BREAKFAST ALREADY SO I HAD COFFEE AND CLAM CHOWDER

I HAVE A MEMORY OF A MOTHER AND HER CHILDREN ALSO EATING AT THE GIFT SHOP. SHE SEEMED TO BE REALLY SET ON MAKING MEMORIES. SHE WAS ODDLY FORMAL WITH THEM, BUT OTHERWISE THERE WAS NOTHING REALLY VERY MEMORABLE ABOUT THEM. BUT I REMEMBER THEM

WE CROSS PATHS WITH STRANGERS. WE DON'T EVEN INTERACT WITH THEM. I WONDER IF I'LL REMEMBER THESE PEOPLE IN THE FUTURE. WHERE WILL I BE? WHERE WILL THEY BE?

SOME REDWOOD SPECIMENS MAY GROW IN EXCESS OF 300 FEET

A BIT DOWN THE ROAD WE ARRIVED AT TREES OF MYSTERY, A CLASSIC TOURIST TRAP!

THIS IS AMAZING

We need to study these trees and think deeply on the course that nature has taken here. As you continue you will see how the redwood grows its burl and every conceivable formation

CRESCENT CITY, CALIFORNIA TO HARRIS BEACH S.P., OREGON **August 10**

MILL CREEK CAMPGROUND WAS AT THE BOTTOM OF A LONG HILL, A GREAT WAY TO END THE DAY ON THE NINTH, BUT THAT MEANT THAT THIS DAY STARTED BY GOING BACK UP THAT LONG HILL. WE GOT TO HIGHWAY 101 AND CONTINUED CLIMBING. THEN IT WAS ALL DOWNHILL TO CRESCENT CITY. WE EXPLORED TOWN A BIT, ATE AT CRISTINA'S FAMILY RESTAURANT, AND WERE BACK ON OUR WAY TO THE FIRST BIG MILESTONE OF THE TRIP

HARRIS BEACH TO HUMBUG MOUNTAIN **August 11**

AFTER A BIT OF RIDING WE STOPPED AT THE BEACH WHERE THE PISTOL RIVER MEETS THE PACIFIC. WE DREW UNTIL THE WIND STARTED WHIPPING SAND AT US

BACK ON THE ROAD THE WIND WAS IN OUR FACE, BUT AT LEAST WE WEREN'T GETTING SANDBLASTED

"YOU'RE GOING THE WRONG WAY"

WE GOT TO THE TOP OF THE HILL, TURNED A CORNER, AND NOW THE WIND REALLY PICKED UP. IT WAS A STRUGGLE TO GO **DOWNHILL**. IF I HAD STOPPED PEDALING THE BIKE WOULD'VE STOPPED. **DOWNHILL!**

WE STOPPED IN GOLD BEACH FOR A BIG AFTERNOON BREAKFAST AT THE GOLDEN EGG. THEN WE HUNG OUT AT THE LIBRARY FOR A COUPLE OF HOURS HOPING FOR THE WINDS TO DIE DOWN. THEY NEVER DID

*WHY **ARE** WE GOING UP THE COAST?*

WHY DIDN'T WE JUST START IN PORTLAND?

WE PUSHED ON, FINALLY ARRIVING AT HUMBUG MOUNTAIN STATE PARK AT 8:00PM. WE SET UP THE TENT, ATE SANDWICHES, I WENT TO CALL MOM AND DAD FROM A PAYPHONE, I TOOK A SHOWER AND HEADED BACK TO THE TENT

IT WAS PITCH BLACK AND I WALKED RIGHT PAST THE CAMPSITE. I DIDN'T HAVE A FLASHLIGHT. THE ONLY LIGHT I HAD WAS A HEADLIGHT FOR THE BIKE WHICH HAD RUN OUT OF BATTERIES THE DAY BEFORE

ANOTHER CAMPER IN THE HIKE/BIKE AREA SAW MY PLIGHT AND SHINED HIS FLASHLIGHT AS A BEACON. I MADE MY WAY THROUGH THE TREES BACK TO OUR TENT

"THANKS SO MUCH!"

HUMBUG MOUNTAIN TO SUNSET BAY STATE PARK — August 12

WE LEFT CAMP BY 7:30 WITH HOPES THAT AN EARLIER START WOULD GIVE US A JUMP ON THE WIND. IT DIDN'T. IT DID FEEL GOOD TO BE ON THE ROAD IN THE EARLY MORNING SUN THOUGH. WE STOPPED AT THE WHEELHOUSE RESTAURANT IN PORT ORFORD. WE COVETED THE PANCAKES BIGGER THAN THE PLATES THEY WERE SERVED ON, BUT KNEW THAT IF WE ORDERED STACKS WE'D HAVE A HARD TIME GETTING BACK ON THE BIKES. INSTEAD WE SIPPED COFFEE AND CAUGHT UP ON WRITING IN OUR DIARIES

> Oh to be going southward. This would be an amazing day! Once again I have this feeling that Pat is responsible for a decision made without enough information, but it's really our fault for being flippant about planning out directions and routes. Oh, this wind!

FULL OF COFFEE WE WERE READY TO FACE OUR FOE, WIND, AGAIN

ALL DAY THERE WERE A LOT OF BIKERS GOING THE OTHER WAY. WE FIGURED OUT THAT THEY WERE PART OF A SUPPORTED BIKE TOUR OUT OF MINNESOTA. MATT KNEW SOMEONE WHO WORKED FOR THE COMPANY SO WE STOPPED A GUY TO PASS ON GREETINGS TO AMY

"DO YOU KNOW AMY?"

"YES!"

SUNSET BAY TO JESSIE M. HONEYMAN STATE PARK **August 13**

THE WIND WAS STILL IN OUR FACE, BUT SO WAS THE SUN. WE WERE IN GOOD SPIRITS WHEN WE ARRIVED TO FIND A PACKED HIKE/BIKE SITE AT HONEYMAN STATE PARK. AS WE WALKED OUR BIKES IN TO FIND AN OPEN SPOT WE PASSED A SMALL GROUP OF GUYS SITTING AROUND A FIRE. ONE OF THEM NOTICED THE FLAG THAT MATT HAD FOUND ON THE ROAD AND TUCKED INTO THE STRAP ON HIS SLEEPING BAG

WE SEEMED TO HAVE STUMBLED INTO A LATE CENTURY HOBO JUNGLE. IT DIDN'T TAKE LONG TO FIGURE OUT THAT TOM WAS THE HOBO KING. HE TALKED WITHOUT CEASING

ALL OF THE BIKERS WERE CROWDED TOGETHER SO NO ONE WAS SAFE FROM HIS ENDLESS MONOLOGUE

HE REALLY ENJOYED GOING ON ABOUT HOW MUCH POT HE SMOKED ESPECIALLY IF HE GOT THE FEELING THE LISTENER WASN'T COMFORTABLE WITH THE SUBJECT. HE WENT ON AND ON ABOUT IT TO A MIDDLE-AGED C.P.A.

HE EVENTUALLY LOST INTEREST IN US AND WANDERED BACK TO HIS FIRE AND HIS CRONIES

MATT AND I PULLED OUT OUR JOURNALS TO CATCH UP ON WRITING. TOM NOTICED

WE, AND MOST OF THE CAMPERS, TURNED IN, TIRED FROM A DAY OF BIKING. TOM QUIETED DOWN WITH NO STRANGERS TO TALK AT. RON TOOK OVER EMCEE DUTIES. HIS VOICE WAS SLURRED AND ACCENTED. WITH THE DETAILS INDISCERNIBLE IT WAS HARD TO PUT MY FINGER ON IT, BUT THESE WERE VIOLENT, DISTURBING CAMPFIRE STORIES

HONEYMAN STATE PARK TO SOUTH BEACH STATE PARK **August 14**

WE LEFT THE HONEYMAN HOBO JUNGLE AND RODE INTO FLORENCE. THERE WERE NO HEADWINDS AND THE SUN WAS OUT

WE GOT COFFEE AND THEN WE SAW SOOTY BOB'S CHIMNEY CLEANING VAN

THE DAY WAS OFF TO A GREAT START!

NOT A SIMPLE INNER TUBE BLOWOUT THAT WOULD'VE BEEN EASILY FIXABLE BUT A BIG HOLE IN THE TIRE ITSELF. I LEFT MATT BY THE SIDE OF THE ROAD AND RODE BACK INTO TOWN TO FIND A BIKE SHOP. BIKES 101 DIDN'T OPEN UNTIL 10:00. THIS GAVE ME A CHANCE TO CATCH UP ON WRITING DOWN THE THOUGHTS THAT WENT THROUGH MY HEAD AS I WAS RIDING ALONG

I BOUGHT A TIRE AND HEADED BACK TO WHERE I'D LEFT MATT

THE BIKE TIRE REPLACED WE WERE BACK ON OUR WAY. THE HEADWINDS HAD PICKED UP — GUSTING UP TO 40 MILES PER HOUR. IT WAS ANOTHER TOUGH DAY MADE EASIER BY PICKING MARION BERRIES BY THE SIDE OF THE ROAD

THE DAY WAS BRIGHTENED FURTHER WHEN WE MET UP WITH ANOTHER NORTHBOUND BIKER. MARK GARDNER HAD BIKED ALL THE WAY ACROSS THE COUNTRY FROM VIRGINIA AND WAS NOW HEADING UP THE COAST TO ASTORIA, OREGON. WE WOULD BE LEAVING THE COAST SOON, BUT IT WAS NICE TO HAVE A FELLOW BATTLER OF THE WINDS TO SHARE THE JOURNEY, AND A MEAL, FOR AT LEAST THIS DAY

SOUTH BEACH S.P. TO DEVIL'S LAKE STATE RECREATION AREA **August 15**

South Beach State Park was a nice place to wake up in the morning. Damp and foggy, but tranquil. The few other bikers that were there were either friendly or kept to themselves.

We had a short day planned so we ate breakfast and then hung around camp until the park's visitor center opened. They'd have free coffee there.

It was just a short ride to Newport. We'd been right by the coast this whole time, but hadn't really spent much time exploring it. The terrain and scenery had been beautiful, but the physical challenge of biking through it left us with little energy for appreciating it. Now that the wind and hills had finally whipped us into shape we'd be leaving it all behind.

Keiko, the whale from "Free Willy," was living at the Oregon Coast Aquarium at the time. They were preparing him to return to the wild in September of 1998. We didn't go there though. Instead we crossed the Yaquina Bay Bridge.

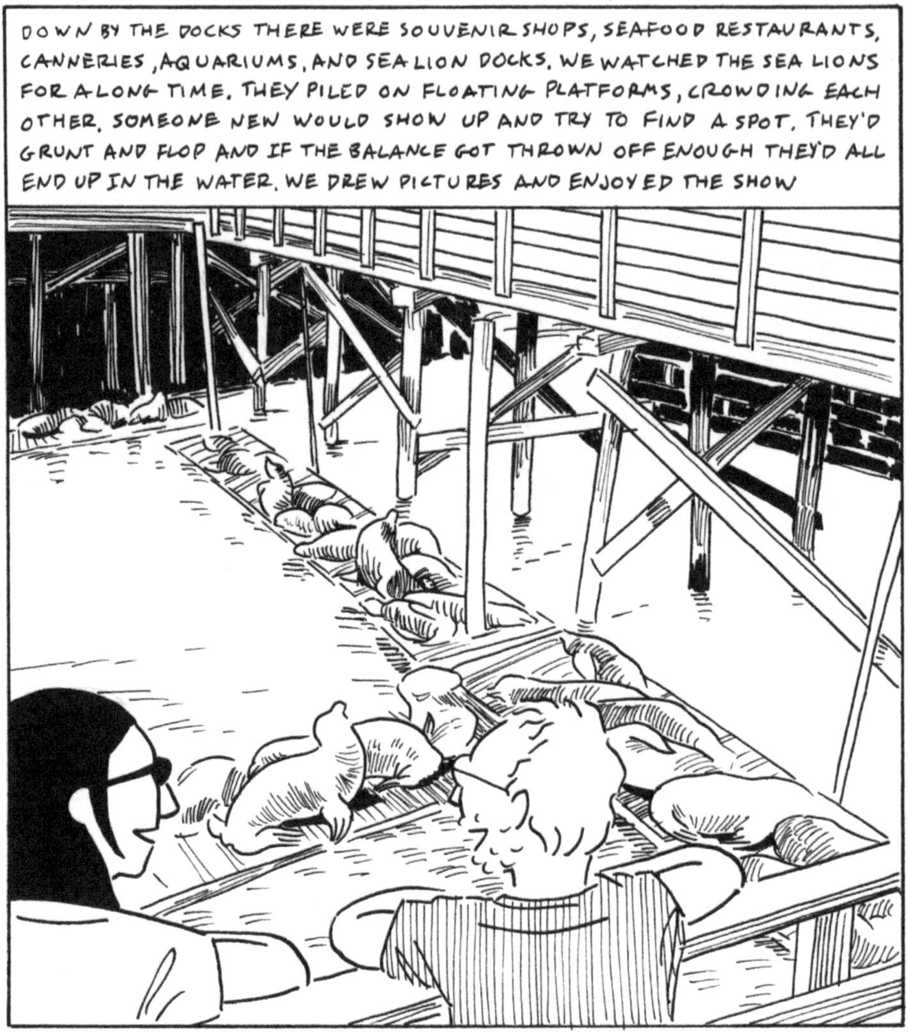

DOWN BY THE DOCKS THERE WERE SOUVENIR SHOPS, SEAFOOD RESTAURANTS, CANNERIES, AQUARIUMS, AND SEA LION DOCKS. WE WATCHED THE SEA LIONS FOR A LONG TIME. THEY PILED ON FLOATING PLATFORMS, CROWDING EACH OTHER. SOMEONE NEW WOULD SHOW UP AND TRY TO FIND A SPOT. THEY'D GRUNT AND FLOP AND IF THE BALANCE GOT THROWN OFF ENOUGH THEY'D ALL END UP IN THE WATER. WE DREW PICTURES AND ENJOYED THE SHOW

CAMPED AT DEVIL'S LAKE STATE PARK THAT EVENING WE HEARD MORE TALES OF SCOUNDRELS ON THE PACIFIC COAST TRAIL

"LOOK OUT FOR AN AUSTRALIAN BIKER NAMED DUGAN McDOWELL"

"HE'S A CROOK"

AS MUCH AS WE'D STRUGGLED DURING THESE PAST TWO AND A HALF WEEKS, CURSING THIS ROUTE THAT WAS A VESTIGE OF PAT'S INVOLVEMENT IN THE INITIAL PLANNING OF THE TRIP, IT WAS GOING TO BE SAD TO LEAVE THE COAST BEHIND

DEVIL'S LAKE TO MCMINNVILLE **August 16**

WE SAID GOODBYE TO MARK. OUR PATHS WOULD NOT CROSS AGAIN. WE PACKED UP AND THEN GOT ON THE ROAD ONLY TO SEE HIS BIKE PARKED OUTSIDE OF A CAFE THREE OR FOUR MILES AWAY. WE WENT IN AND ATE BREAKFAST WITH HIM

AND THEN AT LAST WE WERE ON OUR WAY ACROSS THE COUNTRY. WE EXITED 101 ONTO HIGHWAY 18. RIDING ALONG NEXT TO THE SALMON RIVER A TAILWIND PUSHED US THE WHOLE WAY

ALF'S DRIVE IN DIDN'T HAVE FRIED CHICKEN AFTER ALL, BUT IT DID INDEED HAVE MONKEYS. MONKEYS EVERYWHERE: TOPIARY MONKEYS, CERAMIC MONKEYS, PAINTED MONKEYS, AND TWO REAL LIVE MONKEYS

WE STOPPED AT ROTH'S IGA TO GET MORE FOOD FOR LATER AND FOUND A ROOM AT THE PARAGON MOTEL. $45 WAS MORE THAN WE WANTED TO SPEND, BUT THERE WERE BEDS, WARM WATER, AND "BLUE HAWAII" ON TV

McMINNVILLE TO PORTLAND **August 17**

AFTER A GOOD NIGHT'S SLEEP IN McMONKEYVILLE WE MADE OUR WAY TO PORTLAND. AS WE PASSED THROUGH THE SUBURBS THERE WAS A LOT OF TRAFFIC, BUT FORTUNATELY IT WAS MOSTLY OUTBOUND SO WE HAD THE INBOUND LANES PRACTICALLY TO OURSELVES

SOON WE WERE DOWNTOWN RIGHT IN THE MIDDLE OF RUSH HOUR. WE DISCOVERED THEN THAT THE STORIES OF PORTLAND BEING BIKE FRIENDLY WERE TRUE. THERE WERE LOTS OF BIKE LANES AND THE CARS GAVE US A WIDE BERTH. IT WAS EXCITING TO BE IN A CITY AFTER SO LONG IN THE WOODS AND SMALL TOWNS. WE FOUND SUSAN'S APARTMENT BUILDING IN THE NOB HILL NEIGHBORHOOD WITH NO TROUBLE

HI!

PORTLAND **August 18**

REACHING PORTLAND WAS AN IMPORTANT MILESTONE. IT WAS THE LOCATION WE'D CLAIMED AS OUR FINAL DESTINATION WHEN WE DIDN'T HAVE THE CONFIDENCE TO ADMIT THE TRUTH AND IT WAS THE POINT WHEN OUR CROSS-COUNTRY ENDEAVOR WOULD BEGIN IN EARNEST. WE HAD REALLY LEFT THE COAST NOW! EVEN THOUGH PORTLAND WAS A GREAT BIKING CITY WE WERE PRETTY EXCITED TO GET OFF THE BIKES FOR AWHILE AND REST UP FOR THE CHALLENGES AHEAD

SUSAN WAS A COLLEGE FRIEND OF MY BROTHER'S. SHE HAD JUST MOVED TO PORTLAND, INTERVIEWED FOR A WAITRESSING JOB ON THE 17TH, DIDN'T REALLY KNOW ANYONE IN TOWN YET, AND WAS EXCITED TO HAVE VISITORS TO SEE THE SITES AND TRY OUT RESTAURANTS WITH

MATT STILL REGRETS WE DIDN'T EVER END UP EATING AT THE FISH GROTTO

PORTLAND **August 19**

SUSAN WAS OFFERED THE JOB SHE HAD APPLIED FOR THE DAY WE ARRIVED. NOW TWO DAYS LATER SHE ALREADY HAD ORIENTATION, SO MATT AND I SET OFF ON FOOT TO EXPLORE

WE CLIMBED THE STAIRS, RANG THE BELL, AND A COUPLE OF MINUTES LATER A WOMAN ANSWERED THE DOOR

THE PLACE WAS CRAMMED FULL OF PROPS AND ASSORTED JUNK. SHE RATTLED OFF HER WITTY BANTER LIKE A TOUR GUIDE AT A CAVE, MYSTERY SPOT, OR EVEN GRACELAND ITSELF

A FEW MINUTES INTO OUR PRIVATE TOUR THE DOORBELL RANG

PORTLAND **August 20**

PORTLAND TO HOME VALLEY, WASHINGTON **August 21**

IT WAS SUSAN'S FIRST DAY OF WORK AT HER NEW JOB. SHE WAS UP AND READY TO GO BEFORE WE WERE SO WE SAID OUR GOODBYES, FINISHED PACKING, LOCKED UP AND LEFT

IT HAD BEEN A REALLY NICE BREAK IN THE TRIP. WE KEPT OUR BUTTS OUT OF THE SADDLES FOR A FEW DAYS, SLEPT INSIDE, TOOK WARM SHOWERS, AND ATE WELL. IT HAD BEEN GREAT TO HANG OUT WITH SUSAN AS SHE WAS JUST SETTLING IN TO A NEW HOME. WE WOULD SOON BE IN THE SAME BOAT. I WONDER IF WE OVERSTAYED OUR WELCOME. IF SO SHE NEVER MADE US FEEL THAT WAY, BUT IT COULDN'T HAVE BEEN IDEAL TO BE STARTING YOUR FIRST DAY OF WORK IN A NEW TOWN WITH TWO GUYS IN SLEEPING BAGS ON YOUR LIVING ROOM FLOOR

THERE'S NOT MUCH SPRAWL TO PORTLAND SO WE WERE OUT OF TOWN IN NO TIME. WE NEEDED TO PICK UP SOME BIKE SUPPLIES, BUT WE HAD SHUT OFF OUR BIKING BRAINS SO COMPLETELY WHILE IN PORTLAND THAT WE NEVER SET FOOT IN A BIKE STORE. WE THEN FIGURED WE'D JUST STOP IN A STORE IN VANCOUVER, WASHINGTON, BUT WE BYPASSED THE BUSINESS DISTRICT COMPLETELY. BY THE TIME WE GOT TO CAMAS MATT'S FRONT TIRE WAS ABOUT TO BLOW. LUCKILY WE FOUND A HARDWARE STORE THAT HAD A LIMITED SELECTION OF BIKE SUPPLIES

I SAT ON A BENCH MADE OF 862 RECYCLED PLASTIC MILK CONTAINERS WHILE MATT CHANGED THE TIRE

IT WAS GOOD BEING BACK ON THE BIKES WITH THE WIND AT OUR BACKS

WE CAMPED IN HOME VALLEY. THE COLUMBIA RIVER WAS TWENTY YARDS FROM OUR TENT ON ONE SIDE. ON THE OTHER SIDE WERE RAILROAD TRACKS. WE FELL ASLEEP TO THE SOUND OF THE TRAINS ECHOING THROUGH THE VALLEY

HOME VALLEY TO MARYHILL **August 22**

THE TOUGH BIKING UP THE COAST PREPARED US WELL. THE BIKING WAS A BREEZE NOW!

THE THING WE WEREN'T PREPARED FOR WAS THE LACK OF FOOD AND WATER. TOWNS WERE GETTING FURTHER AND FURTHER APART AND THEY DIDN'T ALL HAVE SERVICES. WE'D NEED TO START PLANNING AHEAD IN A WAY WE HADN'T HAD TO WORRY ABOUT ON THE COAST

SAM HILL WAS A BIG NAME IN THE PACIFIC NORTHWEST AROUND THE TURN OF THE LAST CENTURY. HE WAS SUPER INTO POURED CONCRETE AND PROMOTING KLICKITAT COUNTY. HE HAD SOME BIG IDEAS TO START ONE O' THEM UTOPIAN COMMUNITIES. HE WAS COUNTING ON PLENTIFUL RAINFALL AND A POPULATION OF QUAKERS TO POPULATE HIS TOWN OF MARYHILL (NAMED FOR HIS WIFE, MARY). HE EVEN PUT IN PAVED ROADS (THE FIRST IN THE PACIFIC NORTHWEST)

IT DIDN'T REALLY WORK OUT. MARY REFUSED TO LIVE IN THE CONCRETE CHÂTEAU HE WAS BUILDING FOR HER. SHE TOOK THE KIDS AND WENT BACK TO MINNEAPOLIS. HE TURNED THE MANSION INTO A MUSEUM INSTEAD. HE NEVER DID MANAGE TO CONVINCE OTHERS OF THE POTENTIAL HE SAW IN THIS BARREN LANDSCAPE. HE DID BUILD A SCALE MODEL OF STONEHENGE OUT OF POURED CONCRETE THOUGH. IT'S BETTER THAN THE OTHER STONEHENGE THOUGH BECAUSE IT'S IN ITS COMPLETE FORM, NOT THE FALLING DOWN, MISSING PIECES VERSION LIKE THEY HAVE IN ENGLAND

MARYHILL TO PLYMOUTH **August 23**

IN SPITE OF KNOWING WE HAD A LOT OF MILES TO COVER WE GOT A LATE START OUT OF MARYHILL. IT DIDN'T MATTER. TAILWINDS OF UP TO 30 MILES AN HOUR MADE UP ANY LOST TIME EASILY

RIDING ALONG AT THE SPEED OF WIND SILENCED THE SOUND OF THE WIND IN OUR EARS. WE FLEW ALONG HEARING ONLY OUR TIRES ON THE PAVEMENT

THERE **WAS** A RESTAURANT HERE

The only remaining business in the town of Plymouth was a mini-mart. The woman working the counter was more than willing to tell us all about the recent fire that had done in the Plymouth Tavern & Cafe

"It was a retired firefighter, of all people, who set the fire"

"And a twelve year old boy helped him"

"This boy is one of 48 children fathered by his good-for-nothing, welfare recipient father"

"All by different women of course"

"Well, they caught these idiots right away, but the owners didn't have insurance, and they're not going to get any money out of the good-for-nothings, so that's it"

We camped at the Army Corps of Engineers campground. It was an oasis in a land of sage and tumbleweeds. We were surrounded by trees and grass. Mere yards away the green was replaced by brown and yellow. The Army had drawn their line in the sand

PLYMOUTH TO WALLA WALLA **August 24**

WE WOKE UP EARLY, STRUCK CAMP AT THE OASIS, AND CROSSED THE RIVER INTO UMATILLA. WE WERE BACK IN OREGON

THE COLUMBIA WAS ON OUR LEFT. ROCKY BLUFFS ROSE UP ON OUR RIGHT

WE CONTINUED ALONG THE RIVER, CROSSED THE BORDER BACK INTO WASHINGTON, AND THEN AT WALLULA JUNCTION WE HEADED EAST ON HIGHWAY 12, LEAVING THE COLUMBIA BEHIND

TRUCK AFTER TRUCK PASSED US. THEIR SLIPSTREAMS PUSHED AND PULLED US. AS WE WERE THROWN AROUND WE CAUGHT WHIFFS OF WHAT THEY WERE HAULING. CARROTS, ONIONS, GARLIC. THE SHOULDER WAS LITTERED WITH SHRIVELED UP CARROTS. THE HEADS OF GARLIC FARED PRETTY WELL SITTING IN THE HOT SUN AFTER GETTING THROWN FROM THE TRUCKS. THE ONIONS DID PRETTY WELL TOO IF THEY MANAGED TO SURVIVE THE IMPACT

We rode into Walla Walla. The grass was green. Trees lined the streets. It was a college town, but the students hadn't returned yet

We found a park to camp in. Another well-watered patch of green. Our fellow campers seemed mainly to be contractors and overly friendly kids

WALLA WALLA TO LEWIS & CLARK TRAIL STATE PARK **August 25**

LEWIS & CLARK TRAIL STATE PARK TO CHIEF TIMOTHY PARK **August 26**

WE GOT AN EARLY START, DETERMINED TO HAVE A BETTER DAY. WE ATE OUR ROUTINE CONTINENTAL BREAKFAST OF YOGURT, BANANAS, AND GRANOLA BARS OUTSIDE OF THE IGA FOODLINER IN DAYTON. BY THE TIME WE GOT TO POMEROY WE WERE READY FOR LUNCH

WE CHATTED WITH THE FRIENDLY RETIREE FOR A BIT AND THEN SET OUT TO EXPLORE THE TOWN

WE SAW AN OLD GARAGE FILLED WITH ANTIQUE GAS PUMPS AND SIGNS

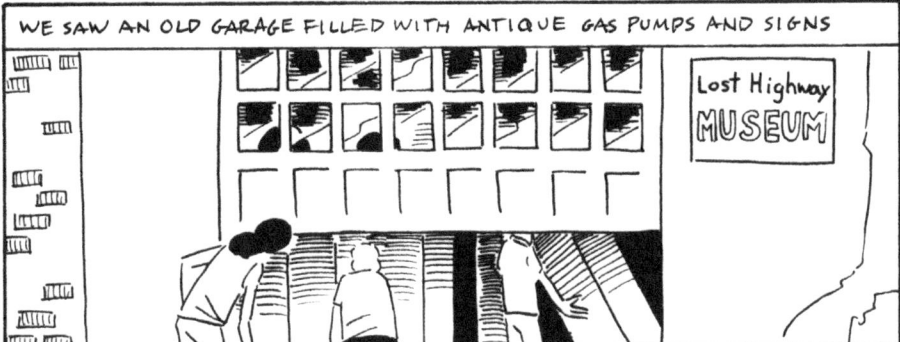

THE OWNER OF THE MUSEUM WAS BUSY MOVING STUFF AROUND. TOO BUSY TO TALK TO US OR SHOW US AROUND. IT SEEMED LESS LIKE A MUSEUM THAN AN ANTIQUE STORE ANYWAY SO WE JUST GOT SOME COFFEE AT THE LOST HIGHWAY CAFE AND THEN GOT BACK ON OUR WAY

ON OUR WAY OUT OF TOWN WE SAW SOME DINOSAURS WELDED TOGETHER OUT OF OLD AGRICULTURAL EQUIPMENT

THE ROLLING HILLS, PERFECT WEATHER, AND A FEW DISTRACTIONS MADE FOR A NICE DAY OF BIKING

WE HAD EXPECTED A TOUGH DAY, BUT IT TURNED OUT TO BE PRETTY FUN

WE MADE IT TO CHIEF TIMOTHY STATE PARK, LOCATED ON AN ISLAND IN THE SNAKE RIVER, BY FOUR. THAT GAVE US TIME TO CHAT WITH A RANGER IN THE INTERPRETIVE CENTER FOR AWHILE AND THEN GO SWIMMING IN THE RIVER

JUST LIKE THAT ALL THE GOOD FEELINGS DISSIPATED AND WE WERE ANNOYED AGAIN

IT WAS TOO DARK AT THE CAMPSITE TO SEE WHAT I WAS WRITING SO I TOOK THE DIARY AND FOUND A STREETLAMP TO SIT UNDER

CHIEF TIMOTHY PARK TO PINK HOUSE HOLE **August 27**

We rode along the Snake River into Clarkston, Washington. We crossed the lift bridge into Lewiston, Idaho and started following the Clearwater River

The brown, rolling hills were gradually replaced by pine-dotted hills. We were heading back into logging country

The scenery was beautiful and it was satisfying to cover the miles by our own effort, but we seemed to have really hit a wall at the four week mark. Our struggle to enjoy the trip continued

PINK HOUSE HOLE TO WILD GOOSE CAMPGROUND **August 28**

WILD GOOSE CAMPGROUND TO POWELL CAMPGROUND **August 29**

WHILE MATT MADE A DRAWING OF HIS PANCAKES I HAD A CHANCE TO WRITE IN THE DIARY A BIT

I DIDN'T WANT TO WRITE ANYTHING YESTERDAY TO AVOID MORE COMPLAINING. AH, BUT TODAY IS A NEW DAY. IT'S SATURDAY MORNING & I JUST HAD PANCAKES, EGGS & HASHBROWNS IN LOWELL, IDAHO AT RYAN'S MOUNTAIN INN

WE STOPPED FOR A LUNCH BREAK AT THE LOCHSA HISTORICAL RANGER STATION AND LOOKED AT THE OLD CABINS AND EXHIBITS

WE ARRIVED AT JERRY JOHNSON CAMPGROUND AND READ THE NOTES POSTED ON THE INFORMATION BOARD

Bears in camp 8/27

bears in camp Aug. 28

IT TURNED OUT THAT BEARS WEREN'T THE REAL PROBLEM WITH JERRY JOHNSON CAMPGROUND THOUGH

"THERE'S NO WATER HERE"

WE BORROWED WATER FROM SOME CAMPERS AND DECIDED WE'D HAVE TO CONTINUE ON TO THE NEXT CAMPGROUND NINE MILES UP THE ROAD. BEFORE GETTING BACK ON OUR WAY WE HAD TO CHECK OUT THE HOT SPRINGS. WE CROSSED THE LOCHSA RIVER ON A SUSPENSION BRIDGE AND HIKED BACK INTO THE WOODS

POWELL CAMPGROUND TO MISSOULA, MONTANA **August 30**

WE WOKE UP, UNEATEN. THE BEARS HADN'T DISTURBED THE FOOD IN OUR STOMACHS OR EATEN THE TOOTHPASTE OFF OUR TEETH

AND THEY HADN'T GAINED ACCESS TO THE FOOD STORED IN THE LATRINE EITHER. THE DAY WAS OFF TO A GOOD START

THE DAY JUST KEPT GETTING BETTER WITH A STOP AT THE LOCHSA LODGE LOCATED NEARBY. I ATE EGGS, HASHBROWNS, AND PANCAKES WHILE MATT DREW HIS PANCAKES

I FINISHED EATING MY EGGS, HASHBROWNS, AND PANCAKES. MATT WAS STILL DRAWING SO I ORDERED A SECOND BREAKFAST OF EGGS, HASHBROWNS, AND PANCAKES. WE WERE ALIVE, THE WEATHER WAS BEAUTIFUL, AND I'D EATEN TWO BREAKFASTS. AN AUSPICIOUS START TO THE DAY

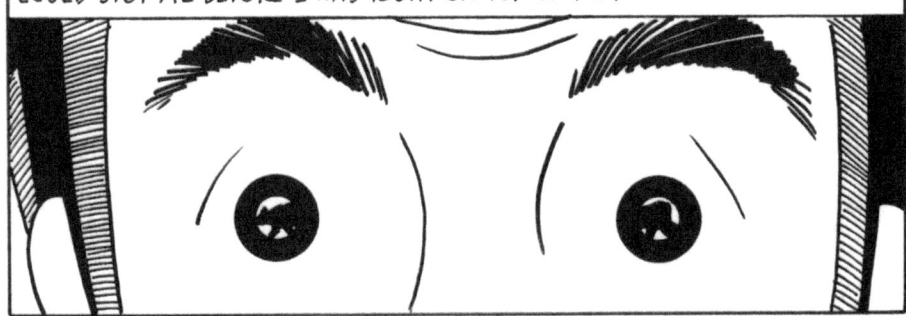

WE MADE OURSELVES AT HOME. FIRST WE STARTED A LOAD OF LAUNDRY AND THEN I JUMPED IN THE SHOWER. I HADN'T HAD A SHOWER SINCE WASHINGTON LET ALONE A HOT SHOWER

WHILE I WAS SHOWERING MATT'S AUNT LOIS, UNCLE LANCE, AND COUSIN LOGAN HAD RETURNED HOME

AFTER EATING OUR FILL OF CANTALOUPE, PIZZA, CHERRIES, AND ICE CREAM WE SLEPT IN BEDS FOR THE FIRST TIME SINCE OREGON

MISSOULA **August 31**

I HAD SO LOOKED FORWARD TO SLEEPING IN A BED, BUT I DIDN'T SLEEP WELL AT ALL. I DREAMED TOO MUCH AND WOKE UP OFTEN

IN SPITE OF THE FITFUL NIGHT'S SLEEP I FELT PRETTY WELL RESTED

WE FINISHED DOING LAUNDRY AND THEN HEADED OUT. WE WANTED A BREAK FROM THE BIKES SO WE WALKED TOWARD A ROAD THAT SEEMED MOST LIKELY TO BE A BUS ROUTE

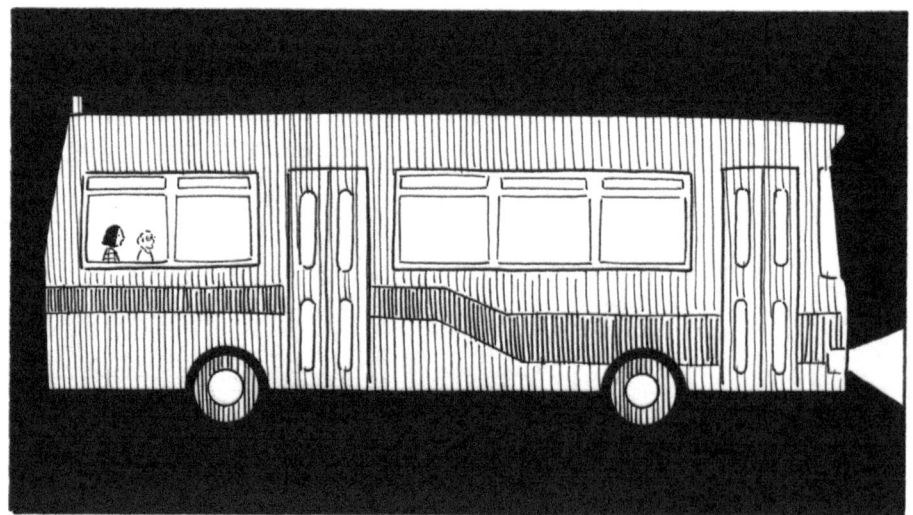

WE'D HAD ENOUGH OF THE GREAT OUTDOORS AND EXERCISING IN IT SO WE DECIDED TO SEEK OUT WHAT THE CITY HAD TO OFFER AND CAUGHT THE BUS DOWNTOWN

AGAIN?

I KNOW, RIGHT? WE REALLY DIDN'T WANT TO BIKE ON A REST DAY DID WE

FIRE ESCAPES, DUMPSTERS, ALLEYS: THIS WAS THE KIND OF STIMULATION WE WERE STARVING FOR OUT ON THE ROAD

WE FEASTED ON ALL THAT CIVILIZATION HAD TO OFFER WITH THE KNOWLEDGE THAT WE MIGHT NOT FIND SUCH BOUNTY AGAIN ANY TIME SOON

"WHOA! THIS THING GOES FAST!"

A THRILLING CAROUSEL RIDE

"THE BRASS RING!"

MATT WON A FREE RIDE

"CHEERS!"

EXOTIC BEERS

"CHEERS!"

"OOH, THAT LOOKS COOL OVER THERE"

MAKING DRAWINGS OF ALLEYS

GONE WITH THE WIND

"I GUESS IT'LL BE COOL TO SEE IT ON A BIG SCREEN"

THERE WERE WARNINGS, INSTRUCTIONS, DIRECTIONS AND ADMONITIONS WRITTEN IN MARKER ON EVERYTHING AND ANYTHING

MISSION MEADOW CAMPGROUND TO COLUMBIA FALLS **September 3**

WE HADN'T GONE FAR BEFORE WE CAME ACROSS A GOOD EXCUSE FOR A BREAK

WE PAID OUR 5 BUCKS AND ENTERED THE SELF-DESCRIBED "SMITHSONIAN OF THE WEST"

"I HAVEN'T BEEN TO THE SMITHSONIAN SINCE I WAS A KID..."

We hope our museum will open enjoyable doors to the past and unlock the secret of the MIRACLE OF AMERICA

"...BUT I REMEMBER IT BEING A LOT BETTER THAN THIS"

THE MIRACLE OF AMERICA MUSEUM HAD A CURATORIAL STYLE AKIN TO A COUNTY HISTORICAL MUSEUM: IF YOU RECEIVE SOMETHING, DISPLAY SOMETHING. THERE'S NO NEED TO WORRY ABOUT CONTEXT—JUST STICK IT IN A CASE OR HANG IT ON A WALL AND YOU'VE GOT AN EXHIBIT

STILL, IT WAS PRETTY FUN LOOKING AROUND AT ALL THE JUNK. THE VIOLANO WAS REALLY COOL, EVEN IF IT WAS REALLY OUT OF TUNE

BUT THEN WE LEFT THE MAIN BUILDING AND ANY ATTEMPT AT CURATION COMPLETELY WENT OUT THE WINDOW

THERE WERE NO MORE EXPLANATORY TAGS OR SIGNS. THE VISITOR WAS LEFT TO COME TO THEIR OWN CONCLUSIONS ABOUT THE MIRACLE OF AMERICA

BY THE TIME WE WERE DONE POKING AROUND THE MUSEUM IT WAS ALREADY LUNCH TIME. WE SAT AND ATE BY THE LAKE IN POLSON AND THEN WE WERE BACK ON OUR WAY

MATT'S PLAN SEEMED TO BE WORKING UNTIL WE WERE JUST SOUTH OF BIG FORK. A BIG CLOT OF TRUCKS WHIZZED PAST US. THERE WAS NO SHOULDER SO WE WERE FORCED OFF THE PAVEMENT. MATT HIT A ROCK AND WHAT HAD BEEN A SLOWLY DEFLATING TIRE BECAME A QUICKLY DEFLATING TIRE

COLUMBIA FALLS, WHITEFISH, AND KALISPELL September 4

IN 1996 MATT HAD LIVED WITH HIS AUNT NORMA AND UNCLE CHUCK. HE WORKED AT THE DAILY INTER LAKE IN KALISPELL. THIS WAS A BIT OF A HOMECOMING FOR HIM

IT HAD JUST BEEN A MATTER OF MONTHS THAT HE STAYED WITH THEM, BUT IT HAD BEEN AN IMPORTANT FEW MONTHS AS IT WAS HIS FIRST EXPERIMENT IN LIVING OUTSIDE OF MINNESOTA

#

COLUMBIA FALLS AND GLACIER NATIONAL PARK **September 5**

WE WENT IN TO GLACIER NATIONAL PARK WITH NORMA AGAIN, BUT THIS TIME SHE HAD TIME FOR A HIKE BEFORE WORK

THE HIKE TO AVALANCHE LAKE WAS BEAUTIFUL, BUT WHAT WOULD'VE BEEN BREATHTAKING VIEWS WERE OBSCURED BY BREATHTAKING HAZE CAUSED BY THE WILDFIRES WHICH BURNED ALL OVER THE PARK

NORMA LEFT US WITH THE CAR AGAIN WHILE SHE WORKED. WE DROVE UP THE GOING TO THE SUN ROAD TOWARDS LOGAN PASS

"MAN, I'M GLAD WE'RE NOT BIKING THIS"

WE CLIMBED OUT ON A LEDGE, CLOSE TO THE WATER, YET PROTECTED FROM THE SPRAY

COLUMBIA FALLS **September 6**

COLUMBIA FALLS **September 7**

COLUMBIA FALLS TO POINT PLEASANT CAMPGROUND September 8

WITH LABOR DAY OVER IT WAS TIME TO START LABORING AGAIN. REST WAS IMPORTANT, BUT THE DAYS WERE GETTING SHORTER AND WE HAD A LONG WAY TO GO YET. WE BEGAN THE DAY BIKING IN A DRIZZLY RAIN, BUT BY NOON THE SUN WAS SHINING

MATT'S THIRD FLAT OF THE DAY MEANT WE MIGHT NOT MAKE IT AS FAR AS WE HAD HOPED

I'M THANKFUL I HAVEN'T HAD A FLAT YET

MAN, I'D BE FRUSTRATED IF I WERE HIM

IT WAS HIS EIGHTH FLAT OF THE TRIP. THE FLAT ON SEPTEMBER 3 HAD BEEN CAUSED BY A THORN, AND THE FIRST FLAT TODAY WAS A CONTINUING RESULT OF THAT PUNCTURE. THE SECOND HOLE WAS CAUSED BY A TINY BIT OF PIANO WIRE

THIS TIME IT WAS A SMALL SHARD OF GLASS

EIGHT MILES BETWEEN PICKING UP SUPPLIES AND A CAMPGROUND WAS ENOUGH

WE HAD GONE 50 MILES FOR THE DAY AND FELT PRETTY GOOD. WE COULD'VE KEPT GOING FURTHER, BUT HAULING THOSE BEERS AN EXTRA 2.5 MILES TO THE NEXT CAMPSITE ON OUR MAP WOULD'VE BEEN A DRAG

PLUS, POINT PLEASANT CAMPGROUND WAS A GOOD PLACE TO STOP. WE TOOK A SWIM IN THE SWAN RIVER

THE WATER WAS FREEZING COLD. VERY WELCOME AFTER A SWEATY DAY

POINT PLEASANT TO SALMON LAKE STATE PARK September 9

THERE WAS INDEED A MARKET IN CONDON SO WE STOPPED THERE FOR BREAKFAST

CASEY PULLED OUT A ZIPLOC BAG OF POWDER AND TRIED TO POUR IT INTO A BOWL OF GRANOLA. AS HE FUMBLED WITH THE BAG A CLOUD OF DUST SPILLED OUT — THE WIND SCATTERING IT FOR MILES

SALMON LAKE STATE PARK TO LINCOLN **September 10**

WE ATE FIRST BREAKFAST IN CAMP AND THEN AFTER 20 MILES IT WAS TIME FOR SECOND BREAKFAST

OVANDO WAS SET BACK FROM THE HIGHWAY A BIT. IT WAS NICE TO GET AWAY FROM THE ROAD

WE SAT ON THE PORCH SHARING A FOUR PACK OF ASSORTED DOUGHNUTS AND DRINKING COFFEE

"I'M GOING TO SEE IF I CAN SEE ANYTHING THROUGH THE WINDOWS OVER THERE"

Trixi began performing in traveling Wild West shows as a teenager

She even signed up with a show in Australia for a time

She was about as big a star as a roper could get

In 1939 they say she single-handedly saved the Calgary Stampede with her costume: tights below and not much above.

Basically nude for 1939

If the venue was too small to do her act on horse she'd use a unicycle instead

She and her beloved horse Silver Dollar retired from show business and settled back in Ovando. She bought The Brand Bar, which is now the museum

When they were building the highway she saw the writing on the wall and moved her establishment to its current location to be closer to traffic

In 1978 she retired, sold the bar, and moved to California to live with her son, Jack

She was diagnosed with Alzheimer's 14 years ago. The last 11 years have been bad

It was kind of frustrating because she traveled so much

She was a great entertainer

She wasn't such a great mother

We didn't see her for years at a time

But she lived her life, and she did it her own way

TO TRIXI!

LINCOLN TO HELENA **September 11**

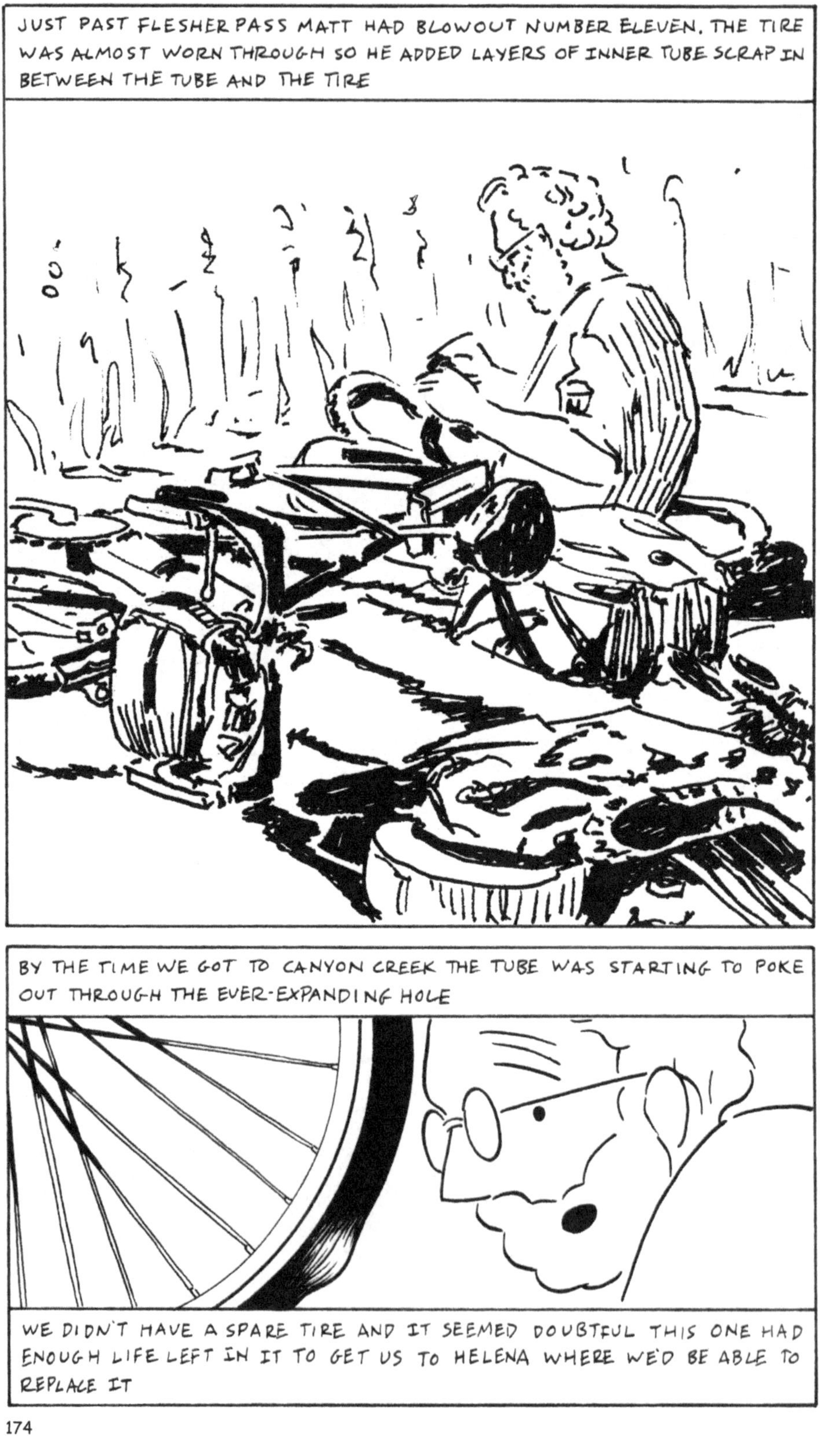

JUST PAST FLESHER PASS MATT HAD BLOWOUT NUMBER ELEVEN. THE TIRE WAS ALMOST WORN THROUGH SO HE ADDED LAYERS OF INNER TUBE SCRAP IN BETWEEN THE TUBE AND THE TIRE

BY THE TIME WE GOT TO CANYON CREEK THE TUBE WAS STARTING TO POKE OUT THROUGH THE EVER-EXPANDING HOLE

WE DIDN'T HAVE A SPARE TIRE AND IT SEEMED DOUBTFUL THIS ONE HAD ENOUGH LIFE LEFT IN IT TO GET US TO HELENA WHERE WE'D BE ABLE TO REPLACE IT

HELENA **September 12**

HELENA TO WHITE SULFUR SPRINGS September 14

WE PUSHED AGAINST THE WIND ALL THE WAY TO TOWNSEND. WE BOUGHT COLD DRINKS AT A GAS STATION AND ATE THE LUNCH WE'D PACKED

AFTER LUNCH THE WINDS DIED DOWN

> WE COASTED EFFORTLESSLY TOWARDS WHITE SULFUR SPRINGS

> MY TIRES WERE THINNER AND LINER-LESS. I WAS FLYING

THE PLAINS, RINGED BY MOUNTAINS, SURROUNDED US

THE STRUGGLES OF THE TRIP FADED AWAY

WHITE SULFUR SPRINGS TO HARLOWTON **September 15**

BEFORE RIDING DOWN THE HIGHWAY WE STOPPED AT THE TOWN'S MUSEUM

"IT'S OPEN"

WE DIDN'T LEAVE TOWN UNTIL ALMOST 1:00

HARLOWTON TO ROUNDUP **September 16**

AFTER A BEAUTIFUL, EASY DAY OF RIDING WE ARRIVED AT ROUNDUP AROUND FOUR. WE KNEW THE NEXT DAY WAS GOING TO BE TOUGH SO WE WERE GLAD TO STOP WITH PLENTY OF THE DAY LEFT FOR TAKING IT EASY

WE WENT INTO A GAS STATION TO ASK THE CLERK IF THERE WAS A PLACE TO CAMP NEARBY

YOU CAN CAMP AT THE COUNTY FAIRGROUNDS

ARE THEY HEAVY?

WHERE ARE YOU GOING?

ARE THESE YOUR BIKES?

WE'D BEEN WORRIED ABOUT THE STRETCH BETWEEN ROUNDUP AND FORSYTH AND NOW WE HAD ONLY ONE SLEEP BETWEEN US AND A 102 MILE DAY

IT WASN'T THAT THERE WEREN'T ANY TOWNS ON THE MAP. MATT HAD DRIVEN THIS STRETCH BEFORE AND KNEW THAT THE TOWNS THAT WERE ON THE MAP WEREN'T REALLY TOWNS

THERE WOULD BE FEW CHANCES FOR WATER SO I FILLED UP THE COLLAPSIBLE CONTAINERS I'D CARRIED ALL THIS WAY. THEY'D HARDLY BEEN NECESSARY BEFORE, BUT NOW THEY MIGHT COME IN HANDY TO KEEP US FROM DYING

ROUNDUP TO FORSYTH **September 17**

I REALLY THOUGHT IT WAS TIME TO GET UP. I SHOULD'VE KNOWN THE GROSS TASTE IN MY MOUTH WAS MORE LIKE THE GROSS TASTE YOU GET IN YOUR MOUTH AFTER A NAP INSTEAD OF THE GROSS TASTE YOU GET IN YOUR MOUTH AFTER A FULL NIGHT'S SLEEP

I MANAGED TO GET BACK TO SLEEP AND STAY ASLEEP UNTIL IT REALLY WAS TIME TO WAKE UP

WE ATE BREAKFAST, PACKED UP, AND STARTED BIKING

THOUGHTS PASSED AND FLOATED AWAY

THEY REPORTED TO US THAT THERE WAS BRIDGE WORK AHEAD IN SOUTH DAKOTA. IT HAD REALLY SLOWED THEM DOWN AND THEY WERE WORRIED ABOUT MAKING IT TO THEIR FINAL DESTINATION BEFORE SNOW FLEW

WE WERE ENJOYING THE OASIS ATMOSPHERE OF THE JERSEY LILLY, BUT IT WAS 2:30 ALREADY. THE SUN WOULD SET IN FIVE HOURS

WHEN THE BATTERIES IN OUR LIGHTS DIED WEEKS EARLIER WE NEVER REPLACED THEM. BATTERIES WERE HEAVY AND THE LIGHTS WEREN'T THAT GREAT ANYWAY. IT WAS BETTER TO JUST BE OFF THE ROAD BY DARK. THERE WAS MORE DARKNESS AND LESS LIGHT EVERY DAY

WE FINISHED OUR BEERS

WE FILLED UP THE WATER BOTTLES

WE LEFT THE BAR WITH FORTY MILES TO GO

A HORRIBLE, WINDY FORTY MILES

THIS SUCKS

THEN, AS NOW, THERE WASN'T MUCH TRAFFIC

BUT A PASSING TRUCK STOPPED AND THE OLD MAN DRIVING IT TOOK HIM THE TWENTY MILES TO FORSYTH TO FILL UP A CAN WITH GAS

AND THEN THE TWENTY MILES BACK TO WHERE MATT'S PICKUP WAS

FORSYTH TO MILES CITY **September 18**

AFTER THE ORDEAL OF THE DAY BEFORE WE WEREN'T IN A HUGE HURRY TO LEAVE CAMP. WE HAD ENDED THE PREVIOUS DAY SO SORE AND SO TIRED—IT WOULD'VE BEEN REAL NICE TO RELAX A BIT AT THE WAGON WHEEL CAMPGROUND, BUT IT WAS ALREADY GETTING HOT AND THE INSECTS WERE SWARMING

AT LEAST WE WERE ONLY TRYING TO GET TO MILES CITY, 46 MILES AWAY. AND IT WAS MAIL DAY!

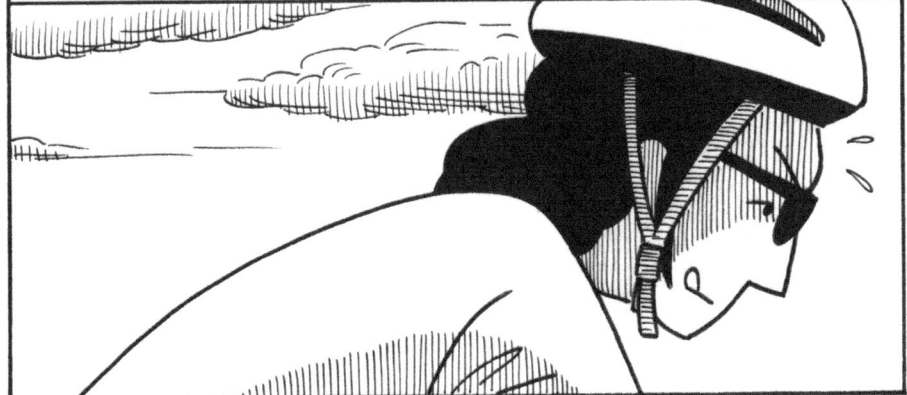

THE DETOUR HAD BEEN ROUGH, NOT ONLY DID IT TAKE HIM A LOT LONGER, BUT WHEN HE STOPPED AT THE LONE GAS STATION ALONG THE WAY HE COULDN'T GET ANY WATER. THE ATTENDANT TOLD HIM LOCALS COULD DRINK IT, BUT NOT HIM. HE'D GET SICK. HE STRUGGLED ON, THIRSTY, ONLY TO FIND THE ROAD EVENTUALLY JOINING UP WITH I-94. HE HAD NO CHOICE BUT TO RIDE ON IT

I'M NOT USUALLY ONE TO SAY, "I TOLD YOU SO", SO I'M SURE I DIDN'T SAY IT

PRETTY SURE

WE LEFT THE TENT-PITCHING FOR LATER AND SET OFF FOR THE POST OFFICE

MAIL DAY!!!

While Matt was at the Range Riders Museum I sat and drew the Range Riders Bar & Casino from a park across the street

The wind started blowing. It blew all the dust from outside of town into town. We got back to camp and struggled to get the tent up

Branches crashed down around us

A boy rode around like the Wizard of Oz witch

We threw everything in the tent and expected we were in for a night of huddling inside of it, trying to stay dry

MILES CITY TO BAKER **September 19**

BAKER, MONTANA TO HETTINGER, NORTH DAKOTA **September 20**

THE WIND THAT HAD PUSHED US ALONG THE DAY BEFORE HAD BROUGHT WITH IT COLDER TEMPS AND GREY SKIES

FORTUNATELY THE PACKAGE I PICKED UP IN MILES CITY INCLUDED A RED TURTLENECK. AWARE THAT COLD WEATHER WAS COMING I'D ASKED MY MOM TO SEND ME A WARM SHIRT

WE FUELED UP AT A DINER BEFORE FACING THE COLD. WE LISTENED IN ON CONVERSATIONS ABOUT THE VIKINGS, A LOCAL KID GOING OFF TO COLLEGE IN MINNESOTA, AND THE FREEZING WEATHER TO COME

"GONNA FROST TONIGHT"

HETTINGER, ND TO McINTOSH, SOUTH DAKOTA September 21

WHEN WE STARTED THE TRIP WE BATTLED WIND AND HILLS WITH UNPREPARED LEGS. THE STRUGGLES MADE IT HARD TO APPRECIATE THE MAJESTIC, NATURAL BEAUTY OF THE COAST AND THE REDWOOD FOREST. WE HAD GOTTEN STRONGER AND STRONGER AND NOW THE BIKING WASN'T SO HARD, BUT THERE WAS NO OCEAN. NO DRIVE-THRU TREES. NO ONE-LOG HOUSES. NO TREES AT ALL REALLY

THERE HAD BEEN TREES. A WHOLE JURASSIC SUBTROPICAL FOREST FULL OF 'EM. DURING THE DEPRESSION SOME INDUSTRIOUS FOLKS TOOK THE PETRIFIED REMAINS OF THAT FOREST AND FASHIONED THEM INTO A GROVE OF STONE TREES

IT WAS A CLEAR, CRISP DAY. THE PETRIFIED WOOD PARK WAS A GREAT PLACE TO SIT AND HAVE LUNCH, BUT IT WAS A BIT TOO COLD TO SIT STILL FOR LONG AND THERE WASN'T ANYTHING ELSE TO SEE SO WE KEPT MOVING

McINTOSH TO MOBRIDGE **September 22**

We woke up to the sound of the McIntosh high school marching band as they marched back and forth past our tent. It felt transgressive to camp in a park right in the center of town, but no one seemed to pay us any mind

We were passing through McLaughlin at lunch time. The Jack & Jill was covered in heavy metal screens. We went in to get something cold to drink

"I wouldn't leave your helmet out there"

"Huh?"

"Why not?"

"I wouldn't leave your helmet out there"

I didn't understand what her problem was, but I went out and got my helmet to appease her

WHEN HE REALIZED WE WEREN'T GOING TO GIVE HIM ANY MONEY HE WANDERED AWAY

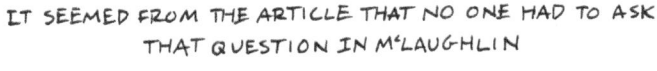

M^CLAUGHLIN IS THE LARGEST TOWN ON THE STANDING ROCK RESERVATION. IN 1998 ITS 800 RESIDENTS SUFFERED HIGH UNEMPLOYMENT AND HIGH CRIME RATES, LOW GRADUATION RATES AND LITTLE OPPORTUNITY. THE WHITES AND THE INDIANS THERE LIVE SEPARATE LIVES. SEPARATE COURT SYSTEMS, SEPARATE POLICE FORCES. THE WHITES ARE ON MOUNTAIN TIME THE INDIANS ON CENTRAL

I FOUND AN ARTICLE FROM FEBRUARY OF 1998 ABOUT A RASH OF SUICIDES THAT HAD HIT THE TOWN HARD. TEENAGED INDIANS WERE KILLING THEMSELVES AT AN ALARMING RATE

WHEN I WAS A KID THERE'D BEEN A TEEN SUICIDE EPIDEMIC IN MY HOMETOWN OF PLANO, TEXAS. PEOPLE ASKED, "HOW COULD THIS HAPPEN HERE?"

IT SEEMED FROM THE ARTICLE THAT NO ONE HAD TO ASK THAT QUESTION IN M^CLAUGHLIN

IPSWICH TO ABERDEEN **September 24**

BLUE CLOUD ABBEY WAS A BENEDICTINE MONASTERY MATT HAD HEARD ABOUT BACK IN COLLEGE. HE KNEW PEOPLE WHO HAD GONE THERE ON WEEKEND RETREATS. WE DIDN'T KNOW TOO MUCH ABOUT IT, EXCEPT THAT BENEDICTINE MONKS WERE KNOWN FOR THEIR HOSPITALITY IN WELCOMING STRANGERS. WE WERE REALLY LOOKING FORWARD TO GETTING THERE. HOSPITALITY SOUNDED AMAZING AND MAYBE THERE'D EVEN BE PEOPLE ON RETREAT THERE FOR US TO MEET. THE ENDLESS PRAIRIE WAS TAKING ITS TOLL ON US. WE NEEDED SOMETHING TO LOOK FORWARD TO

WE ARRIVED IN ABERDEEN AND WERE EXCITED TO BE IN THE FIRST CITY OF ANY SIZE WE'D BEEN IN SINCE LEAVING HELENA. IT WAS A BUSTLING METROPOLIS!

WE POKED AROUND DOWNTOWN A BIT AND SAW THERE WAS A MUSEUM AND THERE WAS ALSO SOMETHING WE'D HOPED FOR THIS WHOLE TRIP

"ALL YOU CAN EAT!!"

YOU BURN THROUGH A LOT OF CALORIES BIKING ALL DAY. WE WERE GOING TO DO SOME SERIOUS DAMAGE

WE ATE PLATE AFTER PLATE OF DECENT CHINESE FOOD. I DEFINITELY GOT MY $4.50'S WORTH

MATT DIDN'T NEED TO BE CONVINCED. I WAS ALWAYS PUSHING TO KEEP MOVING FORWARD AND MATT WAS ALWAYS LOOKING FOR SOMETHING INTERESTING ALONG THE WAY. FINALLY THERE WAS SOMETHING INTERESTING AND I WASN'T TRYING TO GET ANYWHERE

I SOON RECOVERED FROM MY VISION QUEST AND COULD'VE EASILY MADE THE TWENTY MILES MORE TO GROTON, BUT WE'D ALREADY DECIDED TO STAY AND IF WE HAD GONE ON WE WOULD'VE MISSED OUT ON STORYBOOK LAND

ABERDEEN TO BLUE CLOUD ABBEY **September 25**

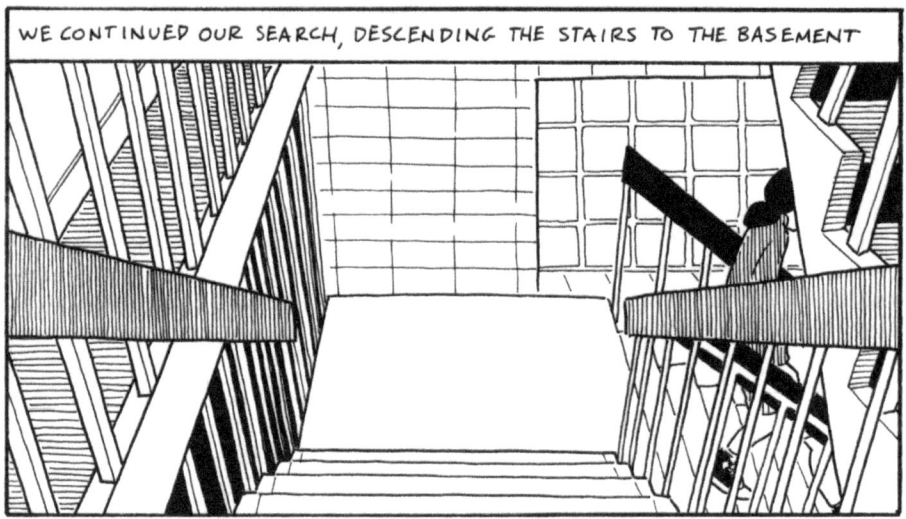

BROTHER SEBASTIAN LED US THROUGH THE KITCHEN INTO ANOTHER, SMALLER DINING ROOM WHERE THE REMAINING FOOD WAS JUST BEING HAULED AWAY ON A CART. WE LOADED UP TRAYS WITH FISH, POTATOES, GREENS, TOMATOES, BREAD AND PUMPKIN PIE.

AFTER PRAYERS BROTHER SEBASTIAN TOOK US TO SEE HIS WORKSHOP

"THIS IS WHERE I SCULPT, PAINT, AND TAILOR"

"I MAKE STOLES, CHAUSIBLES, AND OTHER LITURGICAL VESTMENTS"

"BEAUTIFUL"

"WOW"

BACK IN THE LOUNGE WE CHATTED WITH SEBASTIAN AND SHOWED HIM OUR SKETCHBOOKS

"THESE ARE WONDERFUL!"

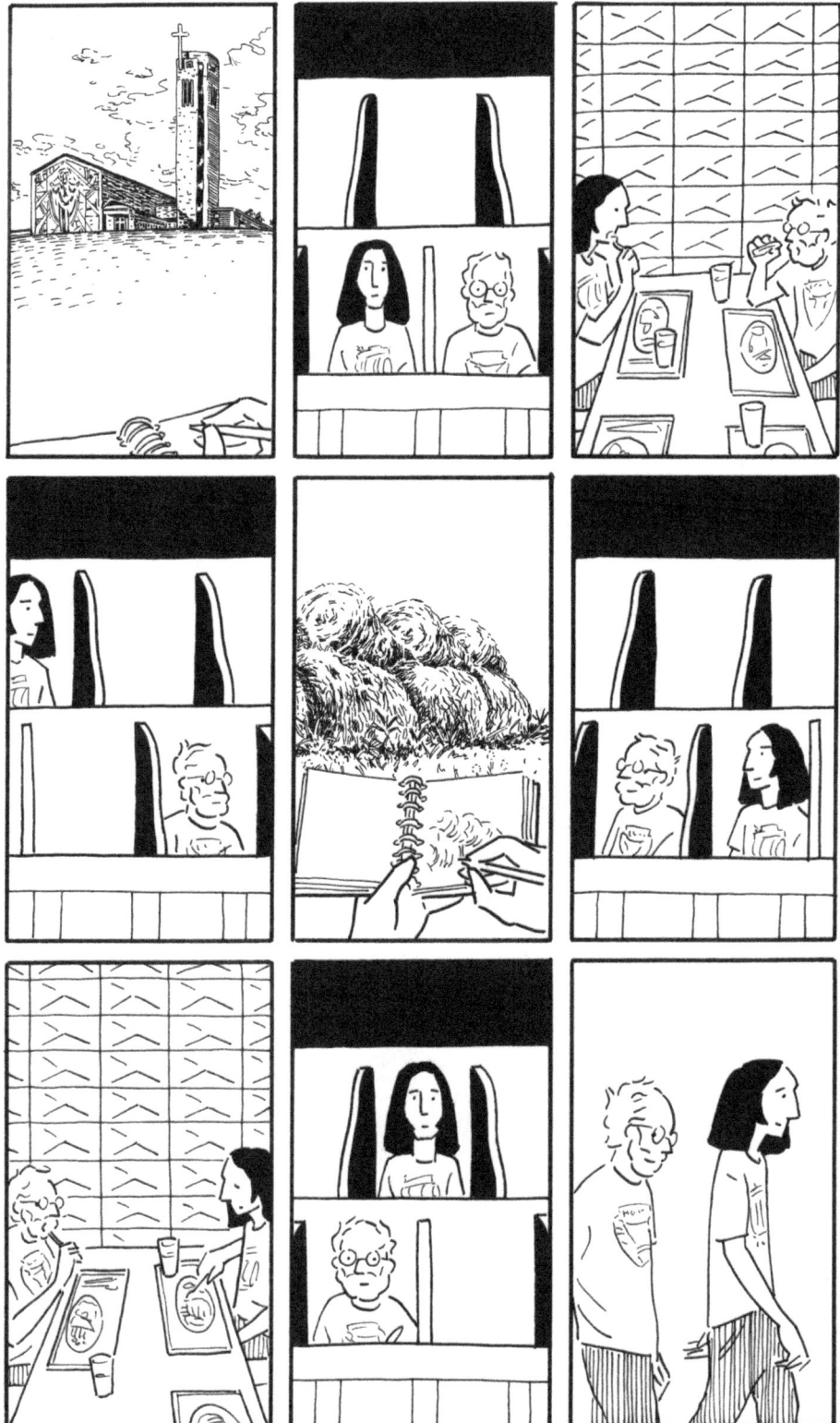

BLUE CLOUD ABBEY TO BENSON, MINNESOTA **September 27**

SUNDAY MORNING AT THE ABBEY. WE'D GET BREAKFAST BEFORE MASS, BUT BEFORE THAT ONE LAST CHANCE FOR MORNING PRAYERS WITH THE MONKS AT 7:30

I KNEW THERE WOULD BE COMMUNION AT MASS. I WANTED TO TAKE PART IN EVERYTHING THIS PLACE HAD TO OFFER, BUT I WAS MINDFUL OF THE FACT THAT I WAS NOT CATHOLIC AND NOT REALLY A PART OF IT

SEBASTIAN, I HAVE A QUESTION ABOUT COMMUNION

IS THERE A POLICY HERE ABOUT NON CATHOLICS COMMUNING?

THAT'S BETWEEN YOU AND GOD

THE SERVICE WAS ATTENDED BY PEOPLE FROM NEARBY COMMUNITIES. THIS WAS THEIR CHURCH

IT HAD BEEN AN ORDEAL GETTING TO BLUE CLOUD ABBEY. WE ARRIVED IN DESPERATE NEED OF REST, FOOD, REFUGE. HAVING RECEIVED THOSE THINGS IN GREAT ABUNDANCE WE SET OFF BLESSED WITH AN EASY RIDE

THE WESTERLY WINDS FROM SATURDAY HAD CONTINUED. THE BIKING WAS EFFORTLESS. THERE WAS NO PHYSICAL STRUGGLE TO DWELL ON — I COULD THINK ABOUT THE GREAT EXPERIENCE WE HAD JUST HAD INSTEAD

MINNESOTA!!!
MINNESOTA!!!

AS WE WERE PUSHED ALONG I THOUGHT ABOUT THE LIVES OF THE MONKS, THE HOSPITALITY THEY SHOWED US, THE COMFORT IN THEIR ROUTINE AND I THOUGHT OF THE GOOFY COLLEGE KIDS, SO EXCITED BY BOX WINE. IT HAD BEEN FUN TO BE AROUND THEM TOO

BENSON TO LITCHFIELD **September 28**

WHAT A DIFFERENCE A STATE MAKES. HIGHWAY 12 HAD A NICE WIDE SHOULDER NOW

THERE WAS A TOWN EVERY FEW MILES. GONE WERE THE WORRIES ABOUT FINDING FOOD AND WATER

WE DIDN'T NEED TO PLAN AHEAD FOR MEALS OR RESORT TO GAS STATION BURRITOS

LITCHFIELD TO MINNEAPOLIS **September 29**

MINNEAPOLIS **September 30**

THERE WAS A DRIZZLING RAIN SO I DECIDED TO PUT OFF RIDING UP TO FOREST LAKE AND JUST STAY AT MATT'S FOR THE DAY. THE BREAK FROM THE ROAD WAS ALSO A BREAK FROM WRITING IN THE DIARY. I DON'T HAVE A DAILY ACCOUNTING OF WHAT WE WERE UP TO DURING THIS TIME—GIVING ME A CHANCE TO CATCH UP ON SOME STUFF I MISSED ALONG THE WAY OR THAT JUST DIDN'T FIT IN

FOR INSTANCE I DIDN'T WRITE ABOUT IT SO I DON'T KNOW WHERE IT HAPPENED, BUT SOMEWHERE IN CALIFORNIA A TRUCK DROVE BY AND THREW TRASH AT US

AND I DIDN'T MENTION THE ONLY CRASH WE HAD. WE WERE STOPPED FIGURING OUT DIRECTIONS IN EUREKA WHEN MATT'S FOOT GOT STUCK IN THE CLIPLESS PEDAL AND HE FELL TOWARDS ME. I GOT TANGLED UP IN MY CLIPS AND WE JUST SLOWLY FELL OVER

FOREST LAKE **October 5**

FOREST LAKE TO MINNEAPOLIS **October 6**

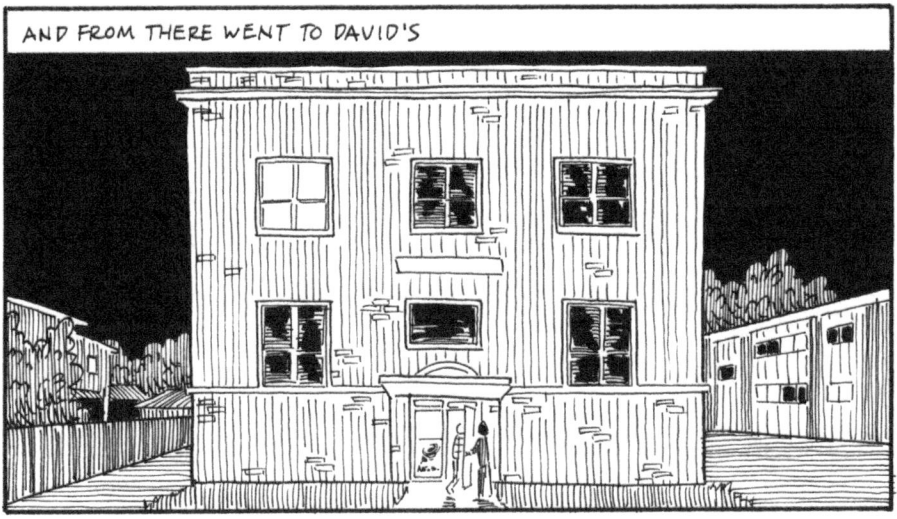

MINNEAPOLIS TO RED WING **October 8**

MR. SITZMANN HAD ALSO BEEN MY BOSS. THE DAY WE LOOKED AT THE APARTMENT HE OFFERED ME WORK AS A PAINTER. WE TOOK THE APARTMENT AND I TOOK THE JOB. HE OFFERED LOTS OF TENNANTS WORK—ESPECIALLY WHEN THE RENTER COULDN'T QUITE AFFORD THE RENT. HE'D TAKE SOME OFF THE RENT IF THEY'D DO A BIT OF YARD WORK OR PAINTING EACH MONTH, BUT WINTER WOULD COME AND THE WORK WOULD DRY UP AND THEY'D START TO RACK UP A DEBT. NOT BEING IN THAT SAME POSITION MYSELF IT EVENTUALLY FELL TO ME TO BE THE FOREMAN OF A CREW OF INDENTURED SERVANTS.

IT STARTED TO GET COLD AND WHEN I TOLD HIM THAT YOU SHOULDN'T PAINT BELOW 50° HE JUST SAID, "THAT'S FOR BEST RESULTS."

EVENTUALLY THE SNOW CAME AND THE INTERIOR WORK HE'D PROMISED NEVER MATERIALIZED. I WAS ALREADY WORKING AS A GUARD AT THE WALKER ART CENTER AND THEN DAVID GOT ME A JOB WORKING WITH HIM AT A WAREHOUSE TO FILL OUT THE REST OF MY SCHEDULE.

AT CHRISTMAS MR. SITZMANN SENT ME A CARD WITH A CHECK FOR 15 DOLLARS. HE NEVER FIRED ME OR LAID ME OFF—JUST IGNORED ME AND THEN SENT THAT STUPID 15 BUCKS

HE WAS A CHARACTER—ENERGETIC AND FRIENDLY—BUT HE ALSO BRAGGED ABOUT HOW HE'D OUTSMARTED THE INSPECTORS WHO'D COME BY TO SEE IF HE WAS FOLLOWING EQUAL OPPORTUNITY HOUSING GUIDELINES. HE WASN'T

ONE TIME HE MADE ME SERVE EVICTION PAPERS TO ONE OF OUR UPSTAIRS NEIGHBORS

SHOULD WE SEE IF HE'S IN THE OFFICE?

NAH. LET'S KEEP MOVING

RED WING TO MERRICK STATE PARK, WISCONSIN **October 9**

A QUICK RIDE BACK ACROSS THE BRIDGE AND WE WERE IN MINNESOTA TO START THE DAY. A BIT LATER AND WE WERE IN WABASHA, HOME OF JOE SUILMAN'S MUSEUM

WE PAID THE ADMISSION PRICE (A QUARTER EACH) AND JOE WALKED US DOWN THE SIDEWALK TO THE GARAGE THAT HOUSED HIS MUSEUM

THE MUSEUM WAS CLOSED, BUT AT LEAST WE COULD LOOK AT THE CEMENT SCULPTURES SURROUNDING IT. HERMAN RUSCH HAD STARTED THE MUSEUM IN 1952 AS A WAY TO KEEP BUSY IN RETIREMENT. BY AROUND 1958 HE DECIDED THE MUSEUM GROUNDS WERE A BIT SPARSE SO HE STARTED SCULPTING IN CEMENT AND MASONRY. OVER THE NEXT 16 YEARS HE CRAFTED A FANCIFUL WORLD OF ROCKETS, HINDU TEMPLES, MOUNTAINS AND DINOSAURS

MERRICK STATE PARK TO NORWALK **October 10**

IT WAS JUST A SHORT RIDE FROM MERRICK STATE PARK TO THE GREAT RIVER STATE TRAIL - LAID ON THE OLD CHICAGO-NORTHWESTERN RAILROAD BED

GREAT RIVER STATE TRAIL

State Trail Pass Required
Before Trail Use

For Bicyclists Ages 16 and Older

Failure to present pass shall result in a surcharge or citation

WE WALKED INTO THE DARKNESS. THERE WAS NO LIGHT AHEAD

THERE WAS NO SOUND EXCEPT FOR THE CLICKING OF OUR GEARS AND THE DRIPPING OF WATER

WE LOOKED BACK TO SEE THE LIGHT FROM THE ENTRANCE GETTING SMALLER AND SMALLER

EVENTUALLY THERE WAS NO LIGHT IN FRONT OF US AND NO LIGHT BEHIND US

WE STOPPED IN THE SENSORY DEPRIVATION CHAMBER FOR A MOMENT BEFORE CONTINUING INTO THE DARKNESS

WE MADE IT TO NORWALK IN THE LAST LIGHT OF DUSK AND SET UP OUR TENT IN THE DARK. THE CAMPGROUND WAS RIGHT ON THE TRAIL AND RIGHT BY TOWN. THERE WERE OTHER CAMPERS AT THE SITE WITH LOTS OF KIDS. THE KIDS WERE LOUD AND UNSUPERVISED

AS WE WALKED INTO TOWN PEOPLE EYED US SUSPICIOUSLY FROM DOORWAYS. GUYS GLARED AT US FROM THE POOLHALL. WE'D SEEN THESE BUSINESSES ADVERTISED ALONG THE TRAIL AND THERE WERE IMAGES OF BICYCLES EVERYWHERE, BUT IT WAS LIKE THEY'D NEVER SEEN A TOURIST

ANOTHER COUPLE OF CAMPERS HAD WANDERED INTO TOWN

A BAR CALLED THE PLACE DEFINITELY LOOKED LIKE IT WAS FOR LOCALS ONLY SO WE WENT TO DIAMOND LIL'S SALOON. MUSIC BLARED WHILE THEY MESSED AROUND GETTING THE KARAOKE MACHINE WORKING

MATT WROTE IN HIS DIARY. I WROTE DOWN TWO HAIKU ABOUT ROADKILL AND THEN JUST SAT THERE, ANNOYED

NORWALK TO MIRROR LAKE **October 11**

WE PRETTY MUCH HAD THE CAMPGROUND AT MIRROR LAKE TO OURSELVES. NOT MANY PEOPLE CAMPING ON A SUNDAY NIGHT IN OCTOBER. WE WERE ABLE TO SCAVENGE ENOUGH WOOD FOR A DECENT FIRE. I WANTED TO STAY NEAR IT AS LONG AS I COULD. IT WAS GOING TO BE COLD IN THE TENT

THE FIRE FINALLY BURNED DOWN TO COALS AND THERE WAS NOTHING TO DO BUT CLIMB INTO COLD SLEEPING BAGS IN A COLD TENT, BUT FIRST WE NEEDED TO DO SOMETHING ABOUT THE GROCERIES

OH, I BET THIS IS TO HANG YOUR FOOD FROM SO THE CRITTERS CAN'T GET TO IT

MIRROR LAKE TO DEVIL'S LAKE **October 12**

WE WERE PRETTY CLOSE TO WISCONSIN DELLS SO WE STRUCK CAMP AND HEADED NORTH FOR SOME TOURISTIC FUN, BUT FIRST WE'D NEED TO REPLENISH OUR FOOD SUPPLY

AFTER A STOP AT A GROCERY STORE WE SAW SOMETHING THAT CHANGED OUR BREAKFAST PLANS: THE SECOND ALL-YOU-CAN-EAT RESTAURANT OF THE TRIP!

"GRANT DELP TOLD ME ABOUT THAT PLACE"

DEVIL'S LAKE TO MADISON **October 13**

I WOKE UP AT FOUR AND HAD TO GO OUT INTO THE COLDEST NIGHT SO FAR. I HAD TO PEE SO BAD I WORRIED THAT MY BLADDER WOULD NEVER GO BACK TO NORMAL AFTER THIS TRIP

I'M NOT SURE EXACTLY WHEN WE ADMITTED TO OURSELVES THAT WE WEREN'T GOING TO MAKE IT ALL THE WAY TO THE ATLANTIC, BUT THESE COLD NIGHTS AND DAYS WERE THE FINAL SAY IN THE MATTER

WE WOULD BE STOPPING IN CHICAGO

MADISON TO DELAVAN **October 14**

WE FOUND THE PATH, TOOK IT, AND THERE OUR TROUBLES BEGAN. THEY HADN'T DONE MUCH TO CONVERT IT FROM A RAILROAD TO A BIKE PATH. IT WAS ALL LOOSE GRAVEL AND WEEDS

IF THEY'D JUST LEFT THE OLD TIES AND RAILS IN PLACE IT WOULDN'T HAVE BEEN ANY WORSE

WE STRUGGLED ON AND MADE IT TO RINGWOOD WHERE WE'D PLANNED ON GETTING FOOD

EXCUSE ME, IS THERE A GROCERY STORE NEAR HERE?

SO WHAT YOU'RE GONNA WANNA DO IS GO DOWN THIS ROAD UNTIL YOU SEE A BIKE PATH AND TAKE THAT

WE STRUGGLED THROUGH RUTTED, LOOSE GRAVEL AND SAND UNTIL WE COULD FINALLY GO NO FURTHER

WE BACKTRACKED AND FOUND OUR WAY ONTO A PARALLEL ROAD

IT LOOKS LIKE IT'S GOING TO GO THROUGH THAT FARM

WE DIDN'T WANT TO GET YELLED AT BY A FARMER, BUT WE ALSO DIDN'T WANT TO DO MORE BACKTRACKING SO WE KEPT GOING

IT WAS JUST A SHORT RIDE BACK TO FOX LAKE, BUT WE SHOULD'VE PASSED BY MUCH EARLIER IN THE DAY IF NOT FOR THAT MISERABLE TRAIL

THE TRAIN TO CHICAGO WAS A THOUSAND FEET FROM THE PATIO MOTEL. WE THOUGHT ABOUT TAKING IT DOWNTOWN AND BACK, BUT DECIDED IT WOULD TAKE AWAY FROM THE THRILL OF OUR PLANNED ARRIVAL THE NEXT DAY. WE WENT TO SLEEP TO THE SOUNDS OF THUMPING BASS FROM THE LAGOON LOUNGE AND THE DRIVE-THRU P.A. OF THE NEIGHBORING TACO BELL

ONE SUPREME GORDITA, ONE CHILI CHEESE BURRITO, AND A LARGE DIET PEPSI

THAT'LL BE $2.83   PULL FORWARD

I GUESS WE FIGURED OUT A WAY TO KILL SOME TIME TODAY

FOX LAKE TO CHICAGO **October 16**

I WAS AWAKE AT 6:15—READY TO GET GOING—BUT IT WAS STILL DARK OUT, MATT WAS SHOWING NO SIGNS OF STIRRING, AND WE DIDN'T HAVE FAR TO GO ANYWAY. I SAT AND LISTENED TO THE CONSTANT RUSH OF TRAFFIC

THE MOTEL WAS RIGHT ON HIGHWAY 12

THE SAME QUIET, LITTLE HIGHWAY WE'D TAKEN THROUGH WASHINGTON...

IDAHO...

MONTANA...

THE DAKOTAS...

AND MINNESOTA

IT WASN'T SO LITTLE OR QUIET ANYMORE

I'D ONLY BEEN TO CHICAGO ONCE BEFORE—A WEEKEND TRIP DURING COLLEGE. THIS WAS ALL NEW TO ME, BUT NOW LOOKING AT OUR ROUTE ON THE MAP I SEE FAMILIAR NAMES AND PLACES

AS WE PEDALED DOWN THE NORTH SHORE ON SHERIDAN ROAD I WAS WITHIN ABOUT A HALF MILE OF EMILY'S HOUSE. IN TWO YEARS I WOULD BE SPENDING A LOT OF TIME THERE

WE STOPPED TO BUY LUNCH AT A JEWEL. EMILY AND I PASS BY HERE ON OUR WAY TO MY MOTHER-IN-LAW'S HOUSE. SOMETIMES I LOOK OVER AND REMEMBER WHEN THIS WAS THE FIRST TIME I'D SEEN A JEWEL

BEFORE GETTING FOOD WE WANTED TO DITCH THE BIKES AT THE BAND LOFT. NOW THAT WE WERE IN THE BIG CITY WE COULDN'T BE SO CASUAL ABOUT LEAVING OUR BIKES UNATTENDED

"WHO ALL LIVES HERE?"

"SAM, JASON, KEVIN, BRIAN"

"SCHOOLEY AND HIS SISTER SARAH TOO"

IT HAD TAKEN US AWHILE TO GET TO THE RESTAURANT. EVERYONE HAD ALREADY ORDERED AND FINISHED EATING. THE STAFF WAS READYING THE ROOM FOR A PRIVATE PARTY

HERE'S THE BILL. I CAN TAKE CARE OF IT AS SOON AS YOU'RE READY

WE WOLFED DOWN AS MUCH ROOM-TEMP PIZZA AS WE COULD BEFORE BEING RUSHED OUT THE DOOR.

"DO YOU NEED MORE CASH?"

"I DON'T THINK I CHIPPED IN ENOUGH"

"NAH, IT'S FINE"

CHICAGO TO DENVER **November 3**

I GUESS THIS IS THE OFFICIAL, NO-DOUBT-ABOUT-IT, END OF THE JOURNEY. FRONTIER FLIGHT 563 JUST ROSE ABOVE THE CLOUDS WEST OF MIDWAY AIRPORT. AS WE CLIMBED AND BANKED IN ORDER TO HEAD IN THE RIGHT DIRECTION I PEERED OUT OF THE WINDOW TOWARDS DOWNTOWN. THE GRID OF LIGHTS EXTENDING OUT FROM IT STARTED TO BE OBSCURED BY A LAYER OF CLOUDS— OFFERING A PEEP SHOW HERE AND THERE OF THE SUBURBAN SPRAWL BELOW. IT WAS 3 AND A HALF MONTHS AGO THAT I WAS WINGING TOWARDS SAN FRANCISCO AND UNCERTAINTY. NOW ALL THOSE MILES ACHIEVED BY MY OWN POWER ARE BEING ERASED BY ANOTHER FLIGHT BACK TO WHERE I STARTED. ALL THAT TIME ON THE ROAD HAS ALREADY STARTED TO BLUR IN MY MEMORY. I THINK BACK ON A SPECIFIC MOMENT, PLACE, OR INCIDENT AND IT'S BECOME A DREAM. UPON OUR ARRIVAL IN CHICAGO WE IMMEDIATELY STARTED A NEW ADVENTURE— FINDING AN APARTMENT

IN A WAY THE MOVE TO CHICAGO IS A CONTINUATION OF THE SAME ADVENTURE. I HAVEN'T REALLY HAD THE CHANCE TO TELL MANY STORIES ABOUT THE TRIP YET, TELLING STORIES IS USUALLY THE WAY I CAN MAKE SENSE OF THINGS THAT HAPPEN. WE DID A LOT OF THINGS AND SAW TONS OF STUFF AND WENT REALLY FAR ON OUR BIKES. DID IT CHANGE ME? I'M NOT SURE YET. I SUPPOSE EVERY MOMENT, EVERY CHOICE LEADS YOU DOWN A PATH THAT THE OPPOSITE WOULDN'T HAVE, BUT WILL THERE BE A MAJOR, NOTICEABLE ALTERATION IN MY LIFE'S PATH? WILL THE TRIP HAVE BEEN A WASTE IF IT DOESN'T LEAD TO SOME BIG CHANGE? MAYBE THE REALIZATION THAT SUCH A SEEMINGLY BIG THING DOESN'T NECESSARILY LEAD TO BIG CHANGES IS THE LESSON. PERHAPS IT WON'T BE A CHANGE IN ME BUT A CHANGE IN THE RELATIONSHIP BETWEEN MATT AND I. I'LL PROBABLY NEVER SPEND SO MUCH TIME, EVERY DAY, FOR SUCH A LONG TIME WITH ONE PERSON

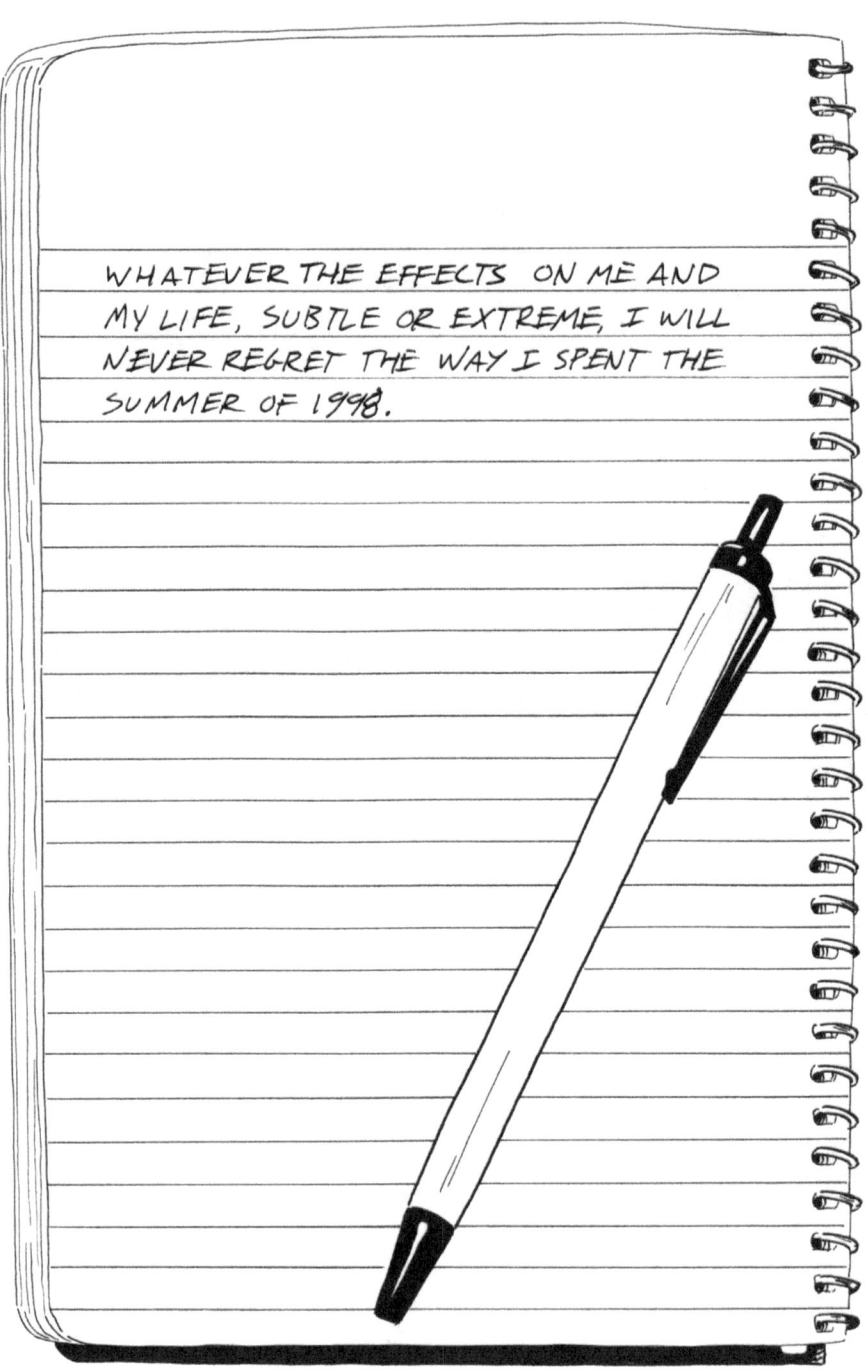

Epilogue

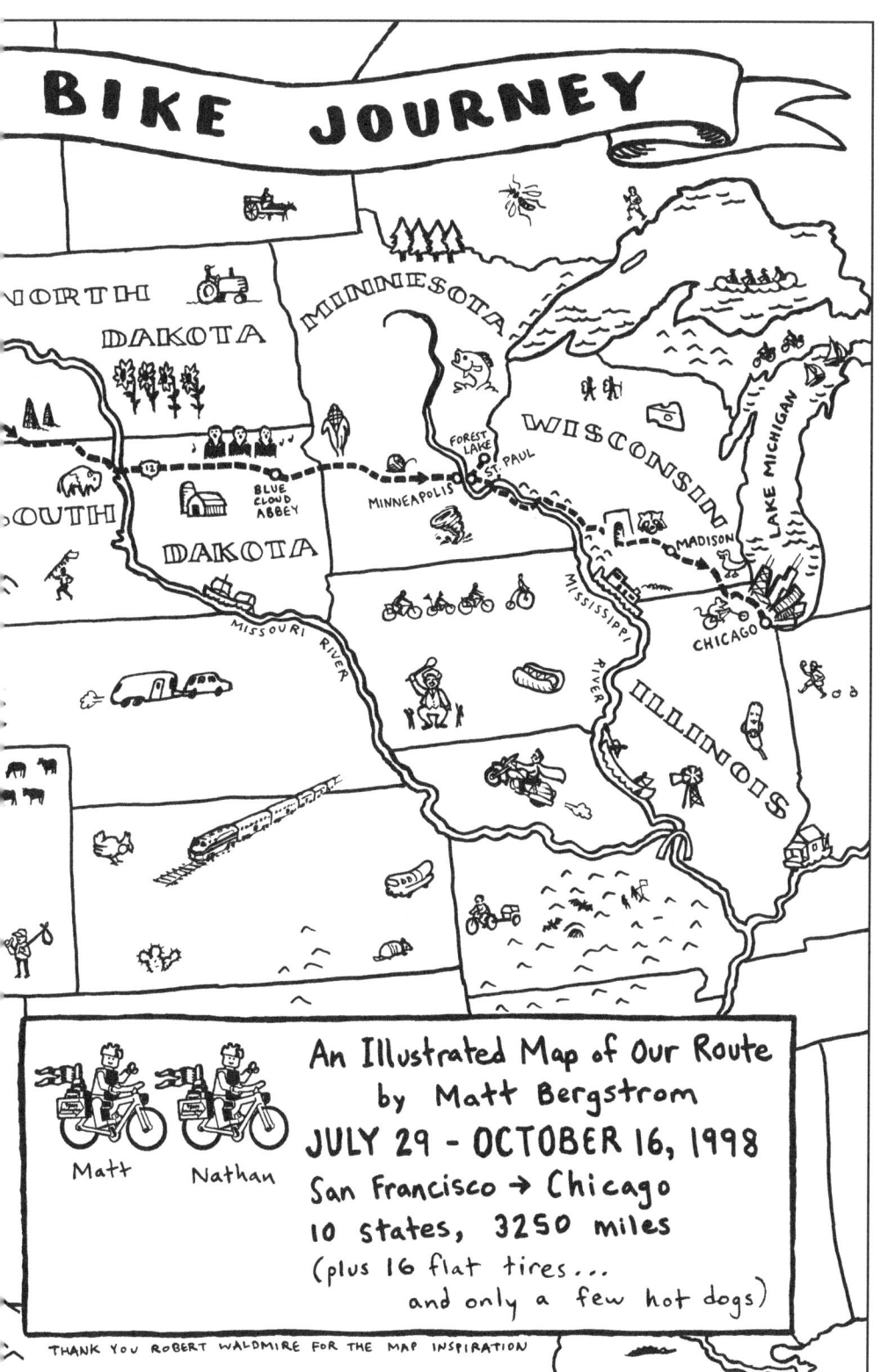